Data Ethics

Data Ethics

How Educators Can Use Data Effectively and Responsibly

Ellen B. Mandinach

BLOOMSBURY ACADEMIC
NEW YORK • LONDON • OXFORD • NEW DELHI • SYDNEY

BLOOMSBURY ACADEMIC

Bloomsbury Publishing Inc, 1359 Broadway, New York, NY 10018, USA
Bloomsbury Publishing Plc, 50 Bedford Square, London, WC1B 3DP, UK
Bloomsbury Publishing Ireland, 29 Earlsfort Terrace, Dublin 2, D02 AY28, Ireland

BLOOMSBURY, BLOOMSBURY ACADEMIC and the Diana logo are trademarks of Bloomsbury Publishing Plc

First published in the United States of America 2025

Copyright © Bloomsbury Publishing, 2025

Cover design by Kathi Ha
Cover images © iStock.com/-VICTOR-

All rights reserved. No part of this publication may be: i) reproduced or transmitted in any form, electronic or mechanical, including photocopying, recording or by means of any information storage or retrieval system without prior permission in writing from the publishers; or ii) used or reproduced in any way for the training, development or operation of artificial intelligence (AI) technologies, including generative AI technologies. The rights holders expressly reserve this publication from the text and data mining exception as per Article 4(3) of the Digital Single Market Directive (EU) 2019/790.

Bloomsbury Publishing Inc does not have any control over, or responsibility for, any third-party websites referred to or in this book. All internet addresses given in this book were correct at the time of going to press. The author and publisher regret any inconvenience caused if addresses have changed or sites have ceased to exist, but can accept no responsibility for any such changes.

Library of Congress Cataloging-in-Publication Data is available

ISBN: HB: 979-8-216-37631-6
PB : 979-8-216-37630-9
ePDF: 979-8-216-37632-3
eBook: 979-8-216-37633-0

Typeset by Deanta Global Publishing Services, Chennai, India

For product safety related questions contact productsafety@bloomsbury.com.

To find out more about our authors and books visit www.bloomsbury.com and sign up for our newsletters.

Dedication

To the two most important men in my life, Eli and Houdi. Your love and support make me a better person. To Eli, who always pushes my thinking and encourages me to be data-driven. To Houdi, for all your feline antics. You both enrich my life daily.

Contents

Acknowledgments ix
Preface xiii

1   An Introduction: Why Data Ethics? 1

2   Defining Data Ethics—It Is More Than Just Data Privacy 11

3   Artificial Intelligence: Implications for Data Ethics 25

4   A User's Guide to the Scenarios 39

5   First Set of Scenarios 53

6   Second Set of Scenarios 117

7   Change Is Systemic—The Roles of Organizations and Agencies 171

8   What Needs to Happen—Actionable Next Steps: A Recap 181

References 189
Index 199

Acknowledgments

My thinking about data ethics has been impacted and informed by many people and events. We live at a time when we are being bombarded by information, misinformation, and disinformation. One would hope that data, information, facts, and evidence form the basis for decision-making, not just in education but in many arenas in life. Sadly, all too often, that is not the case. Denial of evidence is rampant. Individuals need to be able to discern fact from fiction. They need to understand the inquiry process that informs the accumulation and presentation of evidence. Data literacy, information literacy, media literacy, critical thinking, and just plain common sense are all required. Therefore, I would like to acknowledge the media for both good and bad practices. The good can be found in the many articles about protecting yourself from the proliferation of misinformation and disinformation. The bad can be found in the many practices from governmental officials and others that model the dissemination of "alternative facts" and just plain lies. They use the playbook of the illusory effect; if you say something enough times, people will believe it is true. These practices have brought to light the importance of being diligent in terms of using data and information responsibly.

I would like to acknowledge the many educators who struggle to use data effectively and responsibly. They are on the firing line in so many ways and have my utmost respect. They are being asked unknowingly to use a plethora of data and rely on new technologies where the underlying algorithms and databases may have flaws that produce biased results. Educators work under difficult and challenging conditions, but with accountability issues and the context of practice, they may be pressured into using data in ways that may be problematic. They are facing pushback from students and parents who may deny the existence of scientific evidence. I cannot imagine what it must be like to have to calculate what is to be taught and which students might be offended. Educators are on the firing line literally and figuratively. We hear about the negative examples in the media. What we do not hear about are the incredible efforts educators make every day to help their students succeed. They are truly the heroes. I have learned so much from the many educators with whom I have interacted over the years.

I would like to acknowledge the colleagues who have informed my work on the topic of data ethics. First, Edith Gummer with whom I launched the exploration of the topic which led to the edited data ethics book in 2021 (Mandinach & Gummer, 2021b). Our joint work produced the first thinking about what would go into the development of a framework for data ethics (Mandinach & Gummer, 2025). Because this effort was so complex, we sought out the expertise of various colleagues, including Jori Beck, Jo Beth Jimerson, and Laura Hamilton, as we were working to publish the article. In particular, Jori and Jo Beth were amazing thought partners in helping me to consider what a graphical representation of the framework might look like and how it would play out in practice. Their expertise and experience on data, educators, and leaders were invaluable. I would also like to thank my husband, Eli Gruber, for pushing me on the graphical representation to try and make it more understandable. It did not make it into the article, but a version appears in this volume. Other contributors to the 2021 book have stimulated my thinking, in particular Ed Dieterle on technology and artificial intelligence, Sharon Nichols on accountability, Amanda Datnow about equity, and Diana Nunnaley on professional development on data use. Others who have been impactful include Juliana Cotto, Jim Siegl, and Jo Beth Jimerson around our collaborative work on the data privacy scenarios (Mandinach et al., 2021; Mandinach et al., 2023b).

I would like to remember one of my mentors who sadly passed away while I was writing this book. Lee Shulman was a giant in educational psychology. His impact on education will endure. Pedagogical content knowledge was and has been a foundational building block in my thinking about data literacy. Lee's brilliance, humanity, and caring for educators will be missed. Additionally, I would like to acknowledge the other three members of my dissertation committee from long ago whose influence is reflected in this volume: Lee Cronbach on validity and measurement; Lyn Corno on adaptive education, motivation, and instruction; and Dick Snow on aptitude and individual differences. These four individuals helped me to begin my path as an educational psychologist and their influence persists.

I would like to thank my many friends and tennis partners who kept me sane and healthy throughout the writing process. Tennis is such a major part of my life. These people are like a second family to me.

I would like to acknowledge my editors. First, Mark Kerr for encouraging me to write this volume along with the one on culturally responsive data literacy. And then to Nathan Davidson for his editorial assistance and expertise as the book reached fruition.

Finally, and as always, I must thank the two men in my life, Eli Gruber and Houdi. Eli continues to push my thinking and be supportive, although he wants me to write a best-selling book one day! It is not in my repertoire. And Houdi, my ever-present feline research assistant. At least this time you did not add forty pages to the manuscript and ask for a co-authorship and royalties! Houdi puts a smile on my face every day. I could not do this without either of you, so many thanks.

Preface

The topic of data ethics has been emerging as data use has proliferated throughout education. As data use has increased, so too have the diverse sources of data that expand the notion of what data are. No longer are data considered to be only test scores primarily for accountability. There is a pressing need to recognize and use all kinds of data to inform a broad range of decisions. As the kinds of data and the kinds of decisions have broadened, data use has become increasingly complex, thereby creating the need to address issues around ethics. It is no longer sufficient to simply use data effectively; data use must be done responsibly and appropriately.

Ethics are at the heart of all educational practice. Typically, though, ethics are thought of as professionalism and conduct. The National Association of Directors of State Teacher Education and Certification (NASDTEC, 2015, 2023) published the *Model Code of Ethics for Educators* (*MCEE*) that deals with many aspects of professional ethics. The first edition contained principles that were solely focused on teacher professionalism, content, and responsibility to various stakeholder groups. The most recent edition now includes topics that focus on data use. This inclusion signifies that a key professional organization has come to recognize that data ethics have risen to a level of importance for practice. The *MCEE* and other professional standards are explored in Chapter 4.

In conjunction with the proliferation of data, the introduction of technologies to support data use, especially artificial intelligence (AI), has created the need to consider how data are being used not just by educators, but by the vendors and other stakeholders who may have access to the data. Additionally, the underlying algorithms and databases of the technologies have introduced a host of ethical concerns about the appropriateness of the data, the analytics, and of the decisions being made by the technologies. Chapter 3 explores these issues.

Fundamentally, there is a question of what ethical data use looks like and what are the factors that impact appropriate data use. Mandinach and Gummer (2025) posited a theoretical framework with two main components, transparency and consequences, as well as four factors that interact with the components: technical, social, philosophical, and political. The framework is presented in Chapter 2. This framework was part of a collaborative effort with Edith Gummer, where we sought to understand the systemic nature of ethical decision-making. The article that appears in *Teachers College Record* is a first attempt to outline and explore the complexities. The article seeks to raise awareness in the education field about the importance and complexities surrounding ethical data use. It is a first foray to introduce the concept and stimulate discussion. The framework itself is so complex and systemic that we gave up trying to depict it in a graphical representation. Nothing that we drafted accurately captured the interactions among the components in terms of the realities of practice.

The concept of data ethics is part of data literacy; that is, knowing how to use data both effectively and appropriately. As noted in Chapter 2, when data literacy was emerging as a construct and being defined (Data Quality Campaign (DQC), 2014; Mandinach & Gummer, 2016b, 2016c), not enough attention was given to the ethical aspects of data use. Now, it is essential to recognize how ethics impact practice through transparency and the consideration of intended and unintended consequences.

The acquisition and application of data literacy skills and knowledge are not accomplished in isolation. This is about building and sustaining human capacity. It is about creating an infrastructure that supports, nurtures, and values data literacy and data use. This is a systemic issue that involves a number of agencies and institutions. The various roles are explored in Chapter 7. Ethical data use must be modeled, expected, embedded, and enculturated into practice with an explicit vision and a clear understanding of purpose. It takes a coordinated effort from the many stakeholder groups to create a data culture with the technological infrastructure, human capacity, and necessary leadership for effective and responsible data use to occur.

It is the intent of this volume to explore the necessary conditions for such a data culture. It explores the roles and responsibilities for agencies to make this happen. It provides resources to help build human capacity. It also presents a challenge to the field about why data ethics have become essential to educational practice and will continue to grow as new technologies are introduced that push the boundaries around responsible data use.

1

An Introduction: Why Data Ethics?

Chapter Outline

Some Historical Background	1
Professional Ethics and Data Ethics	6
Public Examples	7

Before diving into the meaning and importance of data ethics, I provide a bit of history on the use of data to ground when and how data-driven decision-making has become a topic of interest in education. The chapter briefly discusses professional ethics in contrast to data ethics. It then provides a few examples of how data ethics has become prominent in practice and in public.

Some Historical Background

The use of data and evidence in education became especially prominent in 2002 as the US Department of Education created the Institute of Education Sciences (IES) as an agency to provide sound evidence around educational practice. IES's focus was on the conduct of research, evaluation, and statistics that would aid in decision-making at various levels of the education and political systems. A few years later, two major initiatives were launched to develop a state technology infrastructure and a mechanism for the collection and transmission of data. Hence, the first initiative, in 2005, the Statewide Longitudinal Data Systems (SLDS) Grant Program (n.d.) was created to assist states and territories in building large-scale data systems that could collect, store, and transmit educational data. The intent of these data systems was:

> to enhance the ability of States to efficiently and accurately manage, analyze, and use education data, including individual student records. The SLDSs should help states, districts, schools, educators, and other stakeholders to make data-informed decisions to improve student learning and outcomes; as well as to facilitate research to increase student achievement and close achievement gaps. (p. 1)

The Grants Program has had several rounds of funding, awarding nearly $1 billion to every state and most territories. At first, the awards were focused on building the state data systems for K-12 education and then expanded to early learning through university to workforce. The awards eventually expanded to topics beyond system development such as data usage and educator capacity.

A year after the SLDS Grants program was initiated, IES put into place EdFacts in 2006. EdFacts is seen as what could be considered the data highway, where data are collected at the local level and communicated to the state education agencies and then to the US Department of Education. The data collected through EdFacts are mostly for accountability and compliance purposes to support all sorts of policy-related decision-making.

The combination of EdFacts and the SLDS Grants Program communicated to education the importance of collecting data. What these two programs also communicated was that the technological infrastructure was essential and that there was an almost sole focus on data for accountability. Thus, as data-driven decision-making began to gain traction in the educational sector, most educators, policymakers, and researchers were concerned about several issues. Is there a technological infrastructure to support educational data use? Do educators have access to data? Do educators have access to the "right" or actionable data? Can data use improve student performance? Can educators provide the data needed for local, state, and federal accountability metrics? Many other questions also arose, but most of the early issues focused on accountability and creating the technological infrastructure to make data collection possible.

These foci neglected a key element in the data use equation; that is, educators' ability to use data. It is obviously important to have the technology infrastructure in place, but helping educators to be able to use data effectively must be a parallel and intended outcome. Many questions arise here. Are educators data literate; that is, do they know how to use data effectively? Do educators receive any preparation or training on how to use data in their pre-service experiences or through in-service training? If they do, what is the focus of such training? For educators, what are data? What data are educators trained to use? Is the training basically about how to use the technology to access data from a system or is it about how to actually use the data? Are the data mostly assessment data, or a much broader set of data points? Are there structures in schools and districts to support data use, such as data coaches, data teams, and other needed resources? For what purposes are data being used? How can data help in educational practice? Do data make a difference? Many other fundamental implementation and effectiveness questions existed and continue to persist.

Research and policy focused on these kinds of infrastructure, implementation, and effectiveness questions. For example, IES commissioned a group of five researchers and one practitioner to survey the existing literature to determine what was known about data-driven decision-making in 2009. Over 3,000 documents were reviewed. The outcome was the IES Practice Guide, *Using Student Achievement Data to Support Instructional Decision Making* (Hamilton et al., 2009). A first telling thing about this report is its focus on achievement data, not a broader range of data. IES wanted to ascertain if data-driven decision-making positively impacted student learning, and achievement. This was a mandate from the IES commissioner at that time. A second and delimiting factor was that only rigorous effectiveness research could be included in the literature search, rather than implementation projects. At that time, research was nascent, meaning that implementation was a more prominent focus. Despite those limitations, five recommendations were culled from the then-growing body of research. And these recommendations still are relevant.

1. Make data a part of an ongoing cycle of instructional improvement.
2. Teach students to examine their own data and set learning goals.
3. Establish a clear vision for schoolwide data use.
4. Provide supports that foster a data-driven culture within the school.
5. Develop and maintain a districtwide data system.

Let us consider these recommendations. Data use is an iterative process of inquiry. It is ongoing and continuous, rather than a step-by-step continuum. Even if a decision is reached based on prior data, the outcome of that decision is ultimately fed back into the system for a continuation of the inquiry process. Second, helping students to become their own data-driven decision makers helps them gain co-ownership of the teaching and learning process. Third, it is essential for educators to understand why they are using data and what data they are using. It is therefore critical for building and district leaders to create and communicate an explicit vision for data use. Fourth, there is a need for the establishment of a data culture where data use is expected and data use is modeled by leadership. This includes building leaders providing meeting time for data teams, the provision for data coaches, and other needed supports and resources. Fifth, there is a need for appropriate technologies to support data use. In 2009, the focus was on large data systems, such as data warehouses and student information systems, but now the technologies to support data use are much broader, including data dashboards and all sorts of apps.

Keep in mind that all of this historical introduction thus far has been about a limited scope of data, implementation, and about the effective use of data. For example, the IES Practice Guide (Hamilton et al., 2009) focused only on studies that addressed data related to student achievement, meaning test scores as outcome measures. Improving student performance was the sole criterion for whether data use was "working." Frankly, the issue of improving achievement was premature because there were many foundations to data use not yet in place, most notably educators' capacity to use data.

This situation stimulated a shift toward understanding what it means for educators to be data literate. Beginning in 2011, Mandinach and Gummer (2011, 2013) began a quest to define data literacy so that the construct could be addressed in pre-service and in-service venues to help prepare educators to use data effectively. Although there were a number of books and resources on data use (see Mandinach & Gummer, 2011) available at that time, there were only a few in-service offerings available, and they had limited scope, such as Data Wise (Boudett et al., 2006) and Using Data (Love et al., 2008). Even in the title of the Data Wise books, the sole focus was on using achievement data. Further, attention to data literacy in educator preparation programs was severely limited (Mandinach et al., 2015; Mandinach & Gummer, 2013). If data use was addressed at all, it most likely was found in leadership programs, rather than programs for teachers. Thus, there were several major issues: (a) to expand data use beyond leaders to teachers who use data continuously in their practice; (b) to address the issue of data literacy for all educators; (c) to expand the notion of what educational data are; and (d) to better understand effective data use. Clearly there was a pressing need to broaden the scope of consideration.

Mandinach and Gummer (2016b) continued to address the issue of data literacy. Their effort to define the skills, knowledge, and dispositions needed for educators to be data literate only tangentially touched upon responsible data use. It focused more on effective data use. Over fifty skills, forms of knowledge, and dispositions were identified through a cognitive analysis and in consultation with dozens of experts. In contrast, the Data Quality Campaign (2014) sought to define data literacy in an outwardly focused way so that diverse stakeholders, especially policymakers, could understand what the term meant. This definition did include ethics but lacked any specification about skills and knowledge. I was part of the advisory group and, frankly, was surprised that ethics appeared in the definition. Both of these definitions are laid out thoroughly in Chapter 2. Since those definitions were posed, it has taken several years for the issue of data ethics to emerge and gain traction.

Many factors may have contributed to the shifted attention. First, the emerging technologies have created opportunities for the use and misuse of data. Relatedly, when the pandemic hit, many districts were ill-prepared to move education to a virtual platform. The virtual platform introduced many possible violations of privacy that had to be addressed. Third, the technologies and the lockdown created a need to examine many different forms of data, not just performance data. This need had been brewing, but it became all the more salient, given the move to virtual education. For example, in the wake of the pandemic, the Vermont Agency for Education (2021) laid out its plans for recovery. There were three pillars. The third was to address student performance and learning loss created by the lockdown. But the Agency recognized that there were two precursor considerations. First, they needed to address attendance, truancy, and student engagement. Second, they needed to consider the socio-emotional well-being of both students and teachers. This meant broadening the conception of what data are, well beyond student performance indices. A fourth issue focuses on technologies more generally. Technologies to support data use are necessary. They provide many opportunities for data collection and analysis as well as enhancements to teaching in learning. Yet there is much potential for misuse, including inappropriate data sharing, data breaches, and concerns over security, privacy, and confidentiality. A fifth rationale has emerged as some factions in society have eschewed scientific evidence through the form of denial, perpetuated by the proliferation of misinformation and disinformation (Bergstrom & West, 2020; McIntrye, 2018). The use of data and evidence has been questioned and even rejected, raising the question of how data can be used responsibly, especially when there are individuals that outright reject such use. These issues and others have combined for a perfect storm where there is a need to attend to appropriate data use, not just effective data use.

Professional Ethics and Data Ethics

When ethics are mentioned in terms of educational practice, most often people think of professionalism; what it means to be an ethical professional. Codes of ethics exist for educational leaders and teachers. Most of the tenets laid out in those codes pertain to proper behavior, maintaining professional competence, responsibilities, and proper relationships. For example, the *MCEE* (NASDTEC, 2023) consists of five principles: responsibility to the profession; responsibility for professional competence; responsibility to students; responsibility to the school community; and responsible and ethical use of technology. The InTASC Standards (CCSSO, 2013) contain ten standards. The ninth standard is professional learning and ethical practice. Both of these documents provide broad concepts around what it means to engage in ethical practice. Chapter 4 describes how the two documents address data use and data ethics more specifically. The key difference is that ethics in general are typically about professionalism and behavior. Data ethics focus on how data and evidence are used responsibly to inform practice. Because data are used continuously in educational practice, it is essential to understand the importance of using data appropriately.

Public Examples

Educators are faced with ethical dilemmas all the time. For the most part, educators are well intentioned and if there are violations, they are likely based on a failure to consider the unintended consequences of the decision-making process. Some violations may be completely innocent or blind because educators could be unaware of how data are being collected and used by vendors who have provided technologies to support data use. Violations could be based on not understanding regulations that control student data privacy or confidentiality. Some violations involve individuals beyond the school walls, including parents, higher education, and other stakeholders. Yet some violations could be intended as a way to make a school or district look better in terms of accountability metrics.

To be clear and to reiterate, most educators behave ethically. They have no intention of violating codes of ethics or standards of behavior. But some examples have risen to national awareness that are mentioned here. The intent is to show briefly how things can intentionally or unintentionally go wrong. Some of these examples will be discussed in later chapters and depicted in the scenarios or case studies.

Perhaps the most publicized violation was the cheating scandal that rocked the Atlanta Public Schools. Educators were found to actually change students' answers on standardized tests so that the scores would be better. Arrests and convictions were made. In a second example, but this one at the university level, students at Dartmouth Medical School were accused and initially expelled because their learning management system's data detected potential cheating. The data that were used to make the determination were body and eye movements. These data were flawed, providing an incomplete picture of what the students were actually doing online. A third example was a data breach of a state data system where a vendor acquired information about low-income students and approached them to provide free medical services. A fourth example focuses on how a technology application "outed" a student based on the content of an essay written or the pronouns used in the writing.

Not all data ethics issues involve solely teachers or administrators. A fifth example spans K-12 to higher education and involves parents and university officials. In the Varsity Blues scandal, affluent parents paid stooges to take college entrance tests for their children. They also paid officials, coaches, and administrators at specific colleges and universities to gain acceptance for their children to those institutions.

Further, not all data ethics issues focus on student performance, which is perhaps the most prominent indicator that the general public and policymakers use to determine successful practice. There are a host of accountability measures, such as graduation rate, dropout rate, and the percentage of students accepted to colleges and universities. These metrics can be manipulated. School finance and management data can also be manipulated to make districts look better. Basically, data can always be manipulated in some way, or the presentation of data can be skewed to misrepresent the actual findings. Take, for example, college admissions and the determination of "highly selective" institutions. The goal is to have the lowest percentage of acceptances. There are typically a maximum number of places each year. So the more applicants, the likelihood of lower acceptance rates or higher rejection rates exist. Another key indicator is the yield rate; the percent of students who accept their acceptances. Prestigious institutions seek a high yield rate. All things being equal, they are likely to reject students whom they predict really want to attend another institution. Admissions officers across institutions sometimes will discuss particular applicants and make decisions on such predictions (Selingo, 2020; Toor, 2014).

Even movies and television programs depict ethics in educational settings. *Bad Education* portrays a superintendent and other administrators who embezzle funds, manipulate metrics to make the district look better, and generally conduct district management in an unethical manner. This movie starred Hugh Jackman as the superintendent, one of the few roles where he plays a bad guy. The television series, *English Teacher*, shows cringe-worthy ethical issues that arise in a Texas high school in almost every episode. In one episode, a student divulges that another student has a hidden disease that impacts that student, and the teacher needs to determine how to handle that now public data, including whether it is true or not. The issue here is sharing data with other teachers. In another episode, the teacher has to handle a student who comes to him to seek advice about coming out because the teacher is gay. The *English Teacher* is not the only program to push the limit on ethical behavior. There also is *Abbott Elementary*, a comedy about dedicated teachers trying to help students succeed. In the movie *Gifted*, educators need to determine how best to handle a gifted student. The teacher and the principal disagree about what is best for the student, arguing about nurturing the student's intellectual progress while overlooking the need to address her socio-emotional well-being. This is a whole child issue about what data to prioritize and what is best for the student, given the potential consequences. There are additional complications when family members also disagree about the best course of action, with one individual (the grandmother) focusing solely on intellect and the other (the legal guardian uncle) considering the needs of the whole child. The movie, *Stand and Deliver*, accuses low-income students of cheating on college entrance examinations based on cheating detection metrics at the testing organization. The program determined that these students could not possibly score so well when, in fact, their performance was due to outstanding teaching.

Data ethics abound in daily educational practice. Educators must consider the consequences of their decision-making processes, with the intent to help students and do no harm. Decisions have consequences, so it is important to use the right data and analytics to inform practice.

2

Defining Data Ethics—It Is More Than Just Data Privacy*

Chapter Outline

Providing a Definition	12
Data Privacy	13
A Framework for Data Ethics	14
Linking Data Ethics to Data Literacy	17
Concluding Thoughts	23

This chapter covers a lot of theoretical ground. First, it provides a definition of data ethics. It describes that data ethics are more than just data privacy, about which many educators have familiarity. Because data privacy is so complex, the chapter briefly discusses the topic and provides links to websites where key resources can be found. The chapter then turns to a framework for data ethics, noting that transparency and consequences are the overarching components to consider when using data responsibly. Because data ethics have become such an integral part of data literacy, the chapter then turns to the links between data literacy and data ethics, first providing definitions of data literacy and then noting how the skills,

---

*I would like to acknowledge the contribution of Edith Gummer to the framework. We collaborated on trying to develop this theoretical framework. She eventually withdrew from the process. The framework, however, does reflect some of her ideas as part of the joint development process.

knowledge, and dispositions align with the theoretical framework for data ethics.

Providing a Definition

Put simply, data ethics focus on the appropriate and responsible use of data. Data ethics are about knowing what data and analytics to use, how to draw conclusions and make sound interpretations that can lead to actionable decisions. As the *Forum Guide to Data Ethics* (NFES, 2010) states: "Ethical data professionals never intentionally bias data, manipulate meanings, or otherwise influence interpretation—they present data as accurately and objectively as possible" (p.9). Data ethics typically are equated with the concepts of data privacy and confidentiality. However, the concept is much broader and a foundational part of data literacy (Mandinach & Gummer, 2021b; NFES, 2024). Although many regulations exist around the protection of data, codes of ethics are also relevant here that set standards for proper conduct within the discipline of education. The *Forum Guide to Strategies for Education Data Collection and Reporting* (NFES, 2021) provides insight into both topics: "While laws set the legal parameters that govern data use, ethics establish fundamental principles of right and wrong that are critical to the appropriate management and use of education data" (p. 6).

It is important to keep in mind that data ethics are relevant beyond educational staff. Anyone in a school district who has access to student data has a responsibility to use data appropriately. For example, the director of food services has access to student data about students' families' economic status as they may qualify for free and reduced-price lunches. The transportation director has home addresses and likely information about restraining orders to ensure the safe delivery of students to targeted locations. School nurses have medical information about students. The attendance clerks know who is in school and who is absent. Counselors and school psychologists have knowledge of diverse kinds of data, such as Individual Education Plans (IEPs), disability status, and home status, such as foster care or being sheltered. These are data sources that must be protected.

Data Privacy

When data ethics are mentioned, most educators immediately think of data privacy and data confidentiality. Mandinach and Cotto (2021) define student data privacy as "the responsible, ethical, and equitable collection, use, sharing, and protection of student data" (p. 5). There is no question that data privacy is one of the most critical aspects of using data ethically, but it is only one part. Much attention has been given to the protection of the privacy of student data, and several regulations exist. The law that most directly impacts educators and education is the Family Educational Rights and Privacy Act (FERPA), which lays out the protections for various kinds of student data. FERPA is complex and is constantly evolving. Other regulations that are relevant include the Protection of Pupil Rights Amendment (PPRA), the Children's Online Privacy Protection Act (COPPA), and the Individuals with Disabilities Education Act (IDEA).

There are several key resources where educators can learn more, particularly about FERPA. One is the *Forum Guide to Data Privacy* (NFES, 2016). The Privacy Technical Assistance Center (PTAC), a part of the US Department of Education, provides invaluable resources and training around FERPA and privacy protection more generally. The Future of Privacy Forum (FPF) focuses on aspects of data privacy and has released many resources for educators, including primers and guides (Mandinach & Cotto, 2021; Mandinach et al., 2023a), and scenarios for teachers (Mandinach et al., 2021) and administrators (Mandinach et al., 2023b). FPF's website (https://fpf.org/) and their education-specific site, Student Privacy Compass (https://studentprivacycompass.org/) contain a wealth of helpful resources. Another important source of information about privacy and FERPA can be found from the DQC (https://dataqualitycampaign.org/), a nonprofit that tracks policy trends and key issues around data use. These resources can help educators understand what student data are, the kinds of data that exist (such as personally identifiable information, deidentified data, aggregate data, and metadata), protections, and whom should have access. The resources also deal with potential harms and risks in the event of privacy violations.

Because of the complexity of the regulations around data privacy, it is important for educators to gain an awareness of some of the most fundamental precepts that guide the protection of student data. All educators at all levels have an essential role to play here, from the federal to the state to the local and to the classroom levels. It is important to be clear and transparent, especially when weighing the potential harms and risks. Training educators has become even more important with the emergence of AI. In my opinion, every school and district should include as part of their onboarding process a requirement for FERPA training followed with refreshers. This is something districts have begun to adapt, such as Metro Nashville, where they require FERPA 101 and 102 for all educators (L. Hansen, personal communication, December 15, 2021). Districts need to assume responsibility because data privacy is not a topic typically addressed in pre-service curricula.

A Framework for Data Ethics

To gain an understanding of and appreciation for data ethics, it is helpful to consider the essential components that contribute to the topic. These are foundational concepts that should be considered as all educators use data to inform their practice and make decisions. There are two primary components that have been drawn from my data literacy work as well as from the emerging literature on the use of AI in education that will be addressed in a later chapter. The two components are *transparency* and *consequences*. While transparency was not explicitly part of the data literacy construct, the consideration of the consequences of decisions was, as a skill in the fifth component, *Evaluate Outcomes* (Mandinach & Gummer, 2016b). Transparency is instead, somewhat embedded within the *Use Data* component where there are skills around data quality, selecting the right data, understanding the purposes of data, understanding how to analyze data, and understanding data properties. Thus, both transparency and consequences are grounded within the construct of data literacy. Additionally, data ethics are included as one of the dispositions in data literacy. Educators must have the knowledge, skills, and dispositions that embody data literacy so that data use is both effective and responsible (Mandinach & Gummer, 2016b).

Martin (2022b) defines transparency for data analytics as "providing enough information so that others can understand the performance of the program" (p. 403). Transparency is about being comprehensible to the consumers of the data and information. They must be able to understand the rationale for the decision-making process. The data selection and analytic process must be explicit. Generalizing this, transparency helps to provide explanations that are sufficient to understand how decisions are being made (Holmes, 2023). This involves being clear about what data are being used, what analytic methods are being applied, and the assumptions being made, all in alignment with the intended purposes of the decision-making process (Alwahaby & Cukurova, 2024). Transparency is also about reliability and validity. For reliability, it is about the replicability of the findings and being able to identify issues in the decision-making process, should they arise. For validity, it is about using the appropriate data, the appropriate analytics, and drawing reasonable conclusions for the intended purposes of the decision.

Consequences are the results of the decision-making process. They are outcomes and can be either intended or unintended. For most decisions, there likely are targeted outcomes, objectives that are the focus of the actions taken on the data. However, educators cannot predict all possible outcomes. Actions may not always go as planned, and some things may occur that are not expected. These are the unintended consequences. The concern for such outcomes is that they do no harm or potential damage to students or other levels of the education process. Take, for example, the outing of a student based on writing detection in an app. The consequences can be dire when the school reports its findings to a student's parents who may be unaware of the situation. Major harm can occur.

Validity and reliability come into play around both the transparency and consequences components. Most people think of validity as a characteristic of an assessment; that is, that the test measures what it is intended to measure. Validity and reliability, of course, are technical about using the right data and analytics and being clear about that process and how the decision is being used. But as Cronbach (1988) rightly notes, validity also pertains to the interpretations made from the results, which moves the transparency and technical issues to the consequences. Do the data and results support the conclusions and interpretations? This relates directly to the consequences of the decision. Messick refers to this as consequential validity (Messick, 1989).

Reliability can be a little trickier. One can question if multiple educators look at the same results, will they yield the same interpretations and conclusions? Again, this addresses the consequences. One can hope that is the case, but often times, there could be differing interpretations, in part, due to perspective, expertise, and experience. Take, for example, in medicine, four doctors looking at the same data to make a diagnosis. Those four doctors will apply their areas of expertise and will perhaps make slightly different interpretations based on their specialties. This then becomes an issue of the reliability of the interpretations that can impact the consequences of the decision-making process.

In addition to transparency and consequences, educational decisions are also impacted by other factors, sometimes for the better and sometimes for the worse. These factors include *technical, social, philosophical,* and *political.*

- The technical factor focuses on the analytic and methodological process of decision-making. It includes using the most appropriate data to address the intended purpose of the inquiry. It includes using appropriate analytics and methods to examine the data. It includes issues around data quality, such as reliability, validity, timeliness, completeness, and relevance. The technical factor relates to many of the skills embodied in the second component of data literacy, *Use Data* (Mandinach & Gummer, 2016b) as discussed below.
- The social factor focuses on issues of equity, equality, and diversity among students. It takes into consideration the contexts, backgrounds, and cultures of the students.
- The philosophical factor is about the belief system that influences how educators make decisions. This factor impacts what data are collected and analyzed and the interpretations drawn from that process. Oftentimes, there are unconscious issues that underlie the process, such as educators' assumptions, values, and beliefs. This factor is firmly embedded in the dispositions of data literacy. First and foremost, and also related to the social factor, is the belief that all students can learn. Second is the belief in the use of data to inform practice. Third is the belief that education is a process of continuous improvement. It is not a one-and-done event, but an ongoing cycle of inquiry and improvement.
- The political factor involves the pressures of accountability that surround education and how district and school leadership function within and respond to those pressures (Nichols, 2021). This factor impacts what data may be collected, how they are analyzed, and the

interpretations drawn from the process. The conclusions may or may not be supported by the data, so that the "desired" outcome can be achieved. This factor is about doing the right thing, not yielding to political expedience.

The factors interact with the two components and sometimes conflict with one another. I have struggled to find a way to visually depict the relationships and interactions among the components and factors. Figure 2.1 is an attempt to provide that representation.

Also as a way of showing the complexity of the interactions, Table 2.1 provides examples of how the four factors play out in terms of transparency and consequences.

Linking Data Ethics to Data Literacy

Definitions

Data literacy is an overarching construct of which data ethics are a part. We began working to define a construct called data literacy for teachers (DLFT) in 2011. This construct was based on theoretical work that yielded a cognitive analysis of the skills, knowledge, and dispositions that are required to use data effectively (Mandinach & Gummer, 2016b, 2016c). At that time, data ethics did not explicitly emerge in our definition:

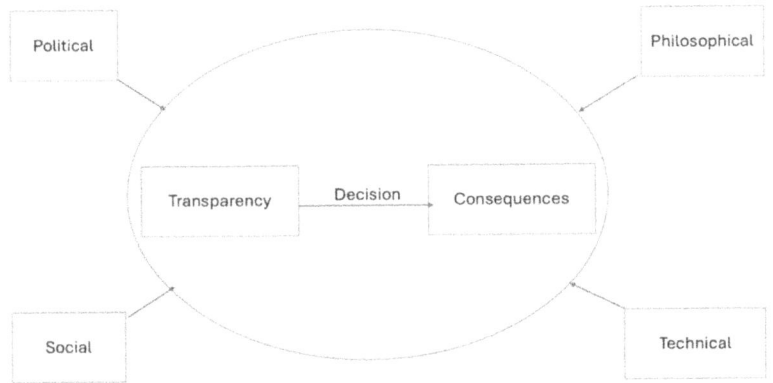

Figure 2.1 The Data Ethics Framework, created by the author.

Table 2.1. The Complex Interactions among the Two Components and Four Factors

	Transparency	Consequences
Technical	Be explicit about the data being used. Question whether they are for the intended purpose. Be explicit about the methodological and analytic processes to be used. Consider the constraints and limitations around the data. Stipulate who is making the decisions, what is to be measured, and for what purposes.	Consider the potential risks and harms based on technical concerns. Be alert to the possible misinterpretations that could result from misuse, applying the wrong data, inappropriate analytics, or drawing unfounded interpretations.
Social	Understand the social and cultural contexts that may impact the decision-making process. Understand the complexities of networked educational levels and the interconnected and possibly competing priorities that may impact decision-making. Understand the importance of equitable learning opportunities for all students.	Understand role-based nature of decision-making; that is, that different stakeholders across the education system may use and view data through their specific lenses and roles. Understand that the outcomes must not disproportionately disadvantage any groups of students intentionally or unintentionally.
Philosophical	Understand the values, belief systems, and the differing perspectives held by various stakeholders within the decision-making process. Be explicit about the beliefs held about students. Be explicit about the importance of using data to inform decision-making.	Understand how belief structures and possible biases may influence the decision-making process. Recognize the potential fallacies and assumptions that could impact decisions both negatively and positively.
Political	Recognize and understand that accountability pressures and compliance may impact the use of data and the decision-making process. Be clear about how those pressures influence the decision-making process.	Understand how policies and structures can and will influence priorities and impact the decision-making process. Recognize that accountability pressures may influence decisions and outcomes for the purposes of political expediency and that those decisions have consequences.

> Data literacy for teaching is the ability to transform information into actionable instructional knowledge and practices by collecting, analyzing, and interpreting all types of data (assessment, school climate, behavioral, snapshot, longitudinal, moment-to-moment, etc.) to help determine instructional steps. It combines an understanding of data with standards, disciplinary knowledge and practices, curricular knowledge, pedagogical content knowledge, and an understanding of how children learn. (Mandinach & Gummer, 2016b, p. 14)

While we were conducting this research, the DQC (2014) sought to provide a succinct and broad definition that would resonate with a variety of stakeholder groups. As part of this working group that developed the definition, I can report that there was lively discussion about the need to include ethics.

> Data-literate educators continuously, effectively, and ethically access, interpret, act on, and communicate multiple types of data from state, local, classroom, and other sources to improve outcomes for students in a manner appropriate to educators' professional roles and responsibilities. (p. 1)

What distinguishes the two definitions is that the DQC included the terms, ethically and appropriate. This was an explicit message to the education community that data use should and must be both effective and ethical. Data ethics could have been highlighted more prominently in DLFT as a skill, but instead, was noted as a habit of mind or disposition.

In the following years, I began to realize that there was more to DLFT than how we had previously defined it. Key research had been conducted that showed that data use marginalized the most challenged students (Datnow, 2017; Datnow & Park, 2018). Furthermore, because data use was so tightly linked to accountability (Nichols, 2021), the discipline tended toward the adoption of three things that created substantial negativity. First, many educators and other stakeholders held a narrow view of what data are, thinking that data are mostly test scores with a direct link to accountability. A much broader perspective was needed by assuming a whole child perspective; that is, students are much more than one test score. Second, data use tended to adopt a deficit model. Data use was about remediating problems and learning deficits, rather than assuming an asset-based approach (Bertrand & Marsh, 2021). Such an approach focuses on students' strengths, interests, assets, and backgrounds.

Relatedly, Bertrand and Marsh (2015) linked attribution theory to data use, showing that when teachers attribute poor performance to non-malleable student characteristics, the attributions become negative. In contrast, attributions to finding different instructional techniques, curricula, or assessment methods can lead to more positive outcomes. Third, equity emerged as a topic of importance. Assuming an equity mindset when engaged in data-driven decision-making can help to ameliorate the marginalization and the deficit modeling (Datnow, 2017). Hence, my work took a philosophical shift that merged culturally responsive teaching (Ladson-Billings, 1995) with data literacy, and hence a newer construct, culturally responsive data literacy (CRDL).

CRDL is defined as follows:

> The ability to use diverse sources of student data and other key data literacy skills to inform decision making about the whole child, using an equity lens and asset-based model to better serve the needs of all children. More specifically, it is the ability to transform information into actionable knowledge by collecting, analyzing, and interpreting diverse data (student performance, socio-emotional, motivation, home context, health, justice, interests, etc.) to help determine instructional steps or inform other educational decisions while taking particular note of the context, background, interests, strengths, and surrounding information of students that may affect their performance and behavior. (Mandinach, 2025, p. 23; Mandinach et al., 2019)

CRDL requires paying attention to the uniqueness of each student. It requires paying attention to the potential for bias and harms. It incorporates the equity mindset, the asset model, and the whole child perspective. Underlying this approach is using data appropriately and responsibly; that is, being ethical.

Linking Data Ethics to the DLFT/CRDL Skills

Theories evolve with the needs of a discipline. Hopefully laying out the definitions above has shown the logical progression toward a more inclusive and broader definition where data ethics are not just assumed but explicit. The DLFT construct contains over 50 skills, knowledge, and dispositions. There are five components that form an iterative inquiry cycle: *Identify Problems/Frame Questions*; *Use Data*; *Transform Data into Information*; *Transform Information into Decision*; and *Evaluate Outcomes*. Note that the first component had a deficit wording. The second and third components contain many of the skills that fall into the technical category and relate to transparency. The fourth component is about pedagogical action, or the decision. The fifth component is about the consideration of consequences of the decision. The dispositions or habits of mind are squarely in the philosophical factor and include data ethics.

An objective here is to link the skills, knowledge, and dispositions specifically to data ethics and the framework noted above. A few do not fit neatly.

- Identify Problems of Practice/Frame Questions
  - Articulate a problem of practice or frame a question—transparency
  - Understand the context at the student level—political and social
  - Understand the context at the school level—political and social
  - Involve other participants and stakeholders—social
  - Understand student privacy—technical
- Use Data
  - Identify possible sources of data—transparency and technical
  - Understand the purpose of different data sources—transparency and technical
  - Understand how to generate data—technical
  - Understand assessment—technical
  - Use formative and summative assessments—technical
  - Develop sound assessment design and implementation—technical
  - Understand data properties—technical
  - Use multiple measures/sources of data—technical
  - Use qualitative and quantitative data—technical
  - Understand the specificity of data to a question/problem—transparency and technical
  - Understand what data are appropriate—transparency and technical
  - Understand data quality—technical

- Understand elements of data accuracy, appropriateness, and completeness—technical
- Understand how to access data—technical (but difficult to categorize)
- Find, locate, access, and review data—technical (but difficult to categorize)
- Use technologies to support data use—technical
- Understand how to analyze data—transparency and technical
- Understand statistics and psychometrics—technical
- Manage data—technical (but difficult to categorize)
- Organize data—technical (but difficult to categorize)
- Prioritize data—transparency and philosophical
- Examine data—technical
- Integrate data—technical
- Manipulate data—technical
- Drill down into data—technical
- Aggregate data—technical
- Disaggregate data—technical

- Transform Data into Information
  - Consider the impact and consequences—consequences
  - Generate hypothetical connections to instruction—consequences
  - Test assumptions—consequences
  - Understand and use data displays and representations—technical
  - Probe for causality—consequences
  - Use statistics—technical
  - Synthesize diverse data—technical
  - Articulate inferences and conclusions—transparency and consequences
  - Summarize and explain data—transparency and consequences

- Transform Information into a Decision
  - Determine next instructional steps—consequences
  - Monitor student performance—consequences
  - Diagnose what students need—consequences
  - Make instructional adjustments—consequences
  - Understand the context for the decision—political, social, and consequences

- Evaluate Outcomes
  - Re-examine the original question or problem—consequences

- Compare performance pre- and post-decision—consequences
- Monitor changes in classroom practices—consequences
- Monitor changes in student performance—consequences
- Consider the need for iterative decision cycles—consequences
- Dispositions
  - Belief that all students can learn—philosophical
  - Belief in data/think critically—philosophical
  - Belief that improvement in education requires a continuous inquiry cycle—philosophical
  - Ethical use of data, including the protection of privacy and confidentiality—technical
  - Collaboration—social and philosophical
  - Communication—social

Concluding Thoughts

This chapter covers a great deal of theoretical ground aimed at providing a foundation for what data ethics are and how they factor into the decision-making process. It is important to keep in mind that data-driven decision-making is an iterative process. It is more about data being collected, analyses conducted, results generated, interpretations made, and actions taken. It is cyclical. As Bergstrom and West (2020) note, data must be "unbiased, reasonable, and relevant to the problem as hand" (p. 43). Thus, data literacy is a critical skill.

The framework for data ethics is meant to stimulate discussion and consideration about the factors that impact any decision in terms of appropriateness and ethics. Decisions are not made in isolation. The key is to be technically sound and transparent about the process and the intentions, with full consideration for the potential consequences, both intended and unintended. This means anticipating possible harms that may result from the decision. However, educational decisions and the data use that leads to those decisions are impacted by factors sometimes beyond the control of educators. This means going beyond the technical aspects of using data appropriately. Belief systems and philosophies are impactful. Social considerations about equity weigh heavily. Perhaps the most pervasive stressor is political, emphasizing the pressures that come from accountability across the levels of the educational system. There are clear pressures for schools and districts to succeed. Public education is at risk with schools closing for financial and performance reasons. Parents pull students and place them in charter, private, or religious schools where there may be a greater chance for success, in their opinion. It can create a negative spiral for public education.

The chapter highlights the importance of data ethics as part of educators being data literate. Thus, it is incumbent upon educators not only to use data effectively but also responsibly. However, there is the issue of ethical literacy and data literacy. Pinski and Benlian (2024) discuss ethical literacy where the focus must be on understanding the data, the models, the risks of actions and being able to discern misinformation, especially in terms of AI.

I have long advocated for the inclusion of data literacy into pre-service education where candidates at least can become familiar with the concepts around data literacy (Mandinach & Gummer, 2013, 2016b). For a variety of reasons, this is difficult, often because pre-service curricula are so demanding and full, so the addition of yet another requirement is often challenging. A survey was administered to the many attendees of the 2016 annual CAEP conference after our keynote address (Mandinach & Gummer, 2016a). Data showed that almost all respondents thought data literacy should be taught at the pre-service level. The preferred method is not a stand-alone course but rather the integration of data literacy into existing courses and experiences (Mandinach & Nunnaley, 2017). Yet we know that data literacy is rarely taught. Dugue and colleagues (2024) also note that digital literacy, focusing on AI is rarely taught. Furthermore, if data literacy is rarely taught, data ethics is even less so addressed (Khodaei et al., 2024). This is a very big issue that needs to be addressed and will be discussed in a later chapter.

I provide some concluding thoughts about the importance of being transparent in the decision-making process and the consideration of the consequences. Data are important, but they are not the panacea. There are limitations and potential risks. Human judgment and experience also have a role to play. Context is important. Educators need to be clear about the data being used and for what purposes. Nguyen (2024) cautions about the limitations of data by noting: "The demand for data-based transparency is an incredibly powerful and effective tool in fighting bias and corruption" (p. 10). There must be a clear balance in data use because over-reliance can be problematic, just as under-reliance can lead to inappropriate conclusions and poor decision-making.

3

Artificial Intelligence: Implications for Data Ethics*

Chapter Outline

AI-Based Technologies	26
Issues Concerning the Model and Framework for AI Use	34
Issues Pertaining to the Decision-Making Process	37
Other Issues	37
Concluding Thoughts	38

The introduction of AI into educational practice has opened up a wide range of opportunities to enhance teaching and learning as well as other educational functions. The power of the technologies was unimaginable only a few years ago. Yet with those opportunities come a plethora of challenges: challenges to practice, challenges to equity, and challenges to ethics. I always talk about the CHOPS—the challenges and opportunities—trying to make the case that the opportunities for data use far outweigh the challenges. D'Souza (2024) notes that many AI experts are warning of potential harms, not just in education but more generally. The concern is that the capabilities are so vast and increasing that in the future, there will be no ability to rein in the technology. As Wang (2019)

---

*I would like to thank the reviewer of the book proposal for suggesting the inclusion of this topic.

so aptly notes, "Data alone do not necessarily lead to wise decisions" (p. 7). A similar argument can be made about technology, including data systems, dashboards, warehouses, and applications. There clearly are risks that must be weighed for educational agencies to understand the balance between the possible negative consequences and the potential for enhancing the teaching and learning process (NFES, 2025). The *Forum Guide to Artificial Intelligence* aptly notes: "Agencies need to be vigilant in monitoring for unintended and negative consequences. Applying ethical judgement that prioritizes the collective good, such as enhanced student learning outcomes, can encourage people to use AI outputs positively" (p. 8). That said, AI raises the stakes to a much higher level. Holmes (2023) summarizes the CHOPS in an understandable manner:

> While AI has the ability to process and analyze vast amounts of data at speeds beyond human capabilities, and while it may mimic intelligent behaviour and sometimes even appears intelligent, it actually lacks consciousness and any real understanding. The fact is that no AI system is capable of replicating the nuanced and complex thinking of human intelligence. (p. iii)

Thus, it is essential that AI be used effectively and ethically.

AI is a rapidly evolving discipline, not only in education but also in society more generally. I do not have a crystal ball, tea leaves, or other projection devices that may predict what AI in education will look like in the future. I can only speak to current policies and practices and the issues that surround the integration of AI into educational practice. Because of the increasing presence in education, it would be remiss to not address some of the ethical challenges that impact its use. Thus, this chapter examines the literature to date around AI. The fact that there are many topics that research and practice have raised should not scare educators away. This chapter discusses various AI applications. The objective here is to raise legitimate concerns and bring awareness to the potential limitations AI has in educational practice.

AI-Based Technologies

Many different kinds of AI-based technologies have emerged and continue to be developed that are being used in educational settings. It is almost like an avalanche of applications that show promise to assist in various ways, not just in the teaching and learning process, but also in educational management and other kinds of structural functions. The purpose of this chapter is not to do a deep dive into the technologies themselves, but rather to introduce some of the technologies that have appeared in the literature where their uses have been highlighted as presenting some ethical concerns.

Concerns around AI-based technologies are emerging. Yet, even some of the simplest technologies that are based in social media pose potential problems. Take, for example, the use of Facebook or Instagram. Posts on these platforms can endanger students and teachers and violate student privacy. Rosenberg and colleagues (2022) raise the issue of data ethics with the proliferation (4.9 million) of pictures being posted on Facebook, where students can be identified through pictures and names.

Personalized Learning

Personalized learning has had more longevity than perhaps other AI-based technologies (Pane et al., 2015). Instructional materials and prompts are generated based on the history of students' responses and the accumulation of various data sources. Based on that history, additional instructional steps are presented to the students to help them progress along a trajectory of expected learning. Holmes (2023) provides a very real caution: "By reducing education to a series of skills, competencies, and outcomes, personalized learning can neglect the holistic development of students and their engagement with the wider world. This reductionist view of education can lead to a narrow focus on test scores and academic achievement, rather than a broader understanding of the value and purpose of education" (p. 62). It reduces the role of the teacher and assumes that the technology uses appropriate pedagogical models. The assumptions may be flawed.

Automated Essay and Machine Scoring

Automated essay and machine scoring systems were instituted many years ago by the major testing organizations to read student essays, for example, for the SAT and TOEFL (Bridgeman et al., 2012; Ramineni et al., 2012). The systems typically use natural language processing to grade work products[1]. The intent was to standardize and objectify the process and remove the potential for human error, subjectivity, and a lack of inter-rater reliability. His intentions were good, but there were unintended consequences. Metrics are often unspecified. The scoring systems check for style, grammar, spelling, intent, coherence, specificity, the use of key words, and content. They make determinations based on the algorithms programmed to determine length and complete sentences, which can disadvantage certain groups of students. The systems have difficulty dealing with non-standard English usage. They may have difficulty dealing with creativity. The systems are programmed to look for essays of a certain length. Some cultures use more elaborated discourse, whereas others use terser language, thereby causing discontinuity in scoring. Additionally, different cultures have different perspectives on students working together or receiving support in their writing, which has a definite cultural component and can lead to bias and potential harm.

Cameras and Facial and Voice Recognition

Facial recognition has become a pervasive technology in society, especially in law enforcement. There are, however, substantial concerns about the balance between security and safety versus privacy, autonomy, and surveillance (Smith & Miller, 2022). In education, facial recognition as well as voice recognition have faced substantial pushback because of allegations of bias underlying the programming and testing. Facial recognition is often used for school ID cards. Voice recognition can be used for teaching and learning. Facial recognition often cannot discriminate among facial features of students and staff of color. The technology also has issues with different ages of faces, skin tones, and gender (Georgopoulos et al., 2021; Lohr, 2023). Voice recognition may not be able to understand individuals with strong accents or have limited English language fluency. If the technologies worked for the intended purposes and had a broader and more accurate dataset to avoid bias and discrimination, then there would be fewer problems.

---

[1] I would also like to thank Cathy Trapani for providing invaluable insights about the nuances of machine scoring from her time at Educational Testing Service.

Issues have arisen. There is great potential for bias in pattern recognition, with the underlying data process being problematic, especially for underrepresented groups. Research has shown that the models tend to amplify bias (Georgopoulos et al., 2021; Serna et al., 2019) with much of the issue being the datasets. Given the issues, research on new models that can improve the datasets and make them more adaptive to improve the fairness metrics is underway (Georgopoulos et al., 2021).

Here are some actual examples. Some schools in Arizona have put into place facial recognition cameras to enhance school safety. The purpose of the cameras is to help educators and resource officers look for irregular or suspicious behavior (Parrish & Sullivan, 2024a, 2024b). The technology notes suspicious behavior and reports it. The cameras can identify parties in fights, too much time spent in a bathroom, or if unauthorized individuals entering the school property. However, there are several concerns, such as misidentification, over-surveillance, unwanted access to the data, and violations of civil rights. The New York State Education Department (New York Office of Information Technology Services, 2023) banned the use of facial recognition in the state's schools. The Department deemed the risks too severe, especially in terms of civil rights. The determination was based on too many false positives for "people of color, nonbinary and transgender people, women, the elderly, and children" (p. 1). However, there are instances in which educators may consider cameras necessary. Heintzelman and Bathon (2017) discuss the use of cameras and surveillance in special education classrooms. Although it is not AI, per se, the intention is for the cameras to detect actions and behaviors where there is potential harm to students. This raises issues of privacy and surveillance and how that counterbalances the need to protect students from harm and abuse.

Voice assistants raise other types of issues beyond the ability of the technology to recognize different accents. Voice assistants help students in their writing, such as crafting complete sentences and using correct grammar. Thus, if there are any irregularities in speech patterns, there might be concerns about the extent to which the technology can accurately process what is being said. Going beyond accents, there could be concerns about what happens if a student has a speech impediment that prevents accurate interpretation. A scoring question might consider what to do if a student does not speak in complete sentences and the assistant corrects this. Similarly, a student may use poor grammar that is corrected. Or cultural speech patterns may differ from what is programmed into the voice assistant. Biases and inaccuracies may occur.

Chatbots

Chatbots are a technology that simulates human conversations. They can write papers and assignments for students. They have emerged as a pervasive presence in education and society more generally. Chatbots can be used to personalize lessons. However, a major concern is around diversity. Like many AI-based technologies, the datasets on which they are based can be a limitation, thereby creating the possibility for bias. Another concern is about the use and production of false or conflicting information (Darling, 2024). A major concern for teachers is how to handle students that have used chatbots to write their assignments for them. There are many ethical questions around this practice. For example, should the use of chatbots be allowed? This practice may not be plagiarism per se, but the work is not technically that of the students. The words are based on AI-generated language. What should a school's policy be around the use of chatbots?

Research conducted in higher education shows both positive and negative aspects in the use of chatbots (Labadze et al., 2023). On the positive side, students receive homework assistance and help in developing targeted skills. For teachers, the technology provides time savings in the form of scoring and other routine tasks. However, concerns were raised about reliability, validity, and accuracy.

Early Warning Systems and Dashboards

There are a number of kinds of warning systems and dashboards that educators can use to alert them to potential issues such as justice and dropouts. Snipes and Tran (2015) conducted a study of the indicators that are most likely associated with the potential for students to drop out. They examined data for 8th grade students in one of the nation's largest school districts and found four indicators: low attendance rate, insufficient credits, low grade point average, and semester Fs. Working with the district, the researchers helped develop a dashboard that the educators could use to alert them to the risk of failure and dropping out if students went off-track in the 9th grade. Students who had more indicators were deemed at a higher risk. The authors also included mindset data such as performance avoidance and embarrassment over failure for consideration. This kind of dashboard is grounded in the collection of data based on research findings. One can question the ramifications of labeling students "at risk" versus providing interventions that may prevent dropping out.

However, Holmes (2023) cautions that the identification of dropouts through AI can be biased. It can unfairly label certain students with discrimination as an unintended consequence. Warning systems are not just used for prediction, such as the probability of dropping out. Bedi and McGory (2020) describe uses related to student justice issues. In another large district, the police have been given access to an early warning system, in conjunction with its own data system, where the data include variables such as curfew violations, custody disputes, and runaways. Students are labeled "at-risk" based on these data as well as others, including the incarceration of a parent, home violence, neglect, abuse, and childhood trauma. There are a number of issues with this kind of data use. First, there is a question of who has the right to access school justice data. Second, there is a question about the appropriate sharing of the data between the school district and the police. Should the police have access to the data? The argument for access stems from the ability to predict and potentially mitigate future incidences of violence. Third, there is a potential for discrimination because some subgroups are more likely to be identified and labeled.

Cheating and Plagiarism Detection and e-Proctoring

Cheating detection became particularly prominent during the lockdown for Covid when educators had to rely on technologies to observe what students were doing during testing periods. The programs rely on detecting abnormal eye movements and body movements as well as click streams. So, for example, if a student reaches for something or looks to the side of the camera, the program might assume that the student was cheating in some way. Someone else might be near the computer or the student might be reaching for a reference or cheat sheet.

The use of e-proctoring systems is not without consequences. Holmes (2023) warns about the analysis of personal data. There can be a negative impact on performance and it can cause excessive stress based on students' knowledge of being watched. Holmes and Tuomi (2022) raise concerns about intrusion, biases, privacy, questions about how the data are being analyzed, and the possible increase in mental health problems due to the surveillance. Further, Holmes (2023) cautions about the use of such technologies more generally: "It can reinforce existing socio-economic and cultural differences, leading to a further marginalization of underprivileged students" (p. 62).

Perhaps the cheating detection incident that gained the most recognition occurred at the Dartmouth Medical School mentioned briefly above. Singer and Krolik (2021) reported that several students were accused of cheating and were expelled based on data from the learning management system being used. The data consisted of both eye and body movements. The interpretations made on this data were flawed. Ultimately the students were reinstated, with the data were deemed flawed or invalid for the particular purpose.

Forms of plagiarism detection have been around for years and have grown more sophisticated over time. Such detection programs have been prominent at the university level but have gained traction in pre-college education. The programs compare written products with databases to determine the level of overlap. For students, the question typically is whether they have copied some reference, online site, or someone else's work product. Plagiarism is serious. It is about the ownership of your own work. Even professionals have gotten caught up in this trap. Take, for example, the allegations against the former president of Harvard University, who was accused of plagiarizing and not providing proper citations for others' work (Schuessler et al., 2024). The individual was forced to resign as president.

Health Applications

Health applications collect a host of biometric data that can be used to monitor if students are healthy, getting enough exercise, and eating nutritionally, among other indicators. Physical education teachers, as well as general education teachers to try and help students understand about the importance of exercise and healthy nutrition. Health applications can be important to students and others who have particular health issues. For example, individuals monitor their biometrics to determine their sugar level for diabetes. Individuals can monitor their heart rhythm to see if they might have an irregular heartbeat, heart rate, or if they are experiencing atrial fabulation, or supraventricular tachycardia. My tennis team all wear Apple watches to track steps, amount run, heart rate, and calories expended during a match. These data can be vitally important when there is a potential for a medical issue. However, biometric data, including data such as fingerprints, are very personal, and critics have raised the issues of surveillance, fear of monitoring, and privacy (Alwahaby & Cukurova, 2024; Buck, n.d.). A question remains if and how educators can use such technology and data while maintaining students' privacy.

Classroom Monitoring

Classroom monitoring uses technology to observe the actions in school settings. According to Holmes (2023), the technology examines facial expressions, body movements, and behaviors such as disengagement to look for irregularities. Clearly, there can be issues of over-surveillance with such technology. Issues of privacy arise. Both students and teachers may be anxious about constantly being watched. Using a non-AI-based example, educators in Arizona raised significant concerns when one of the candidates for governor seriously proposed to install cameras in every classroom to monitor activity and what was being said (Roberts, 2021). This proposal was definitely about surveillance, censorship, and a violation of student privacy. Most educators were adamantly opposed to the idea. However, some saw it as a way to protect themselves if accusations were leveled about having said or done something about which a student complained. They saw it as a means to provide concrete evidence. Regardless of the intentions, the negative consequences for classroom monitoring may far outweigh the positives.

Deepfakes

Deepfakes are not a part of the educational process, but their existence and proliferation have and will continue to plague educational institutions. Deepfakes occur when an individual takes a photo or video of someone and edits the visuals through the use of AI to create a completely fake representation. The perpetrator uses face-swap technologies to accomplish the goal. What has happened is a student will superimpose the head of another student or a teacher on the nude body from an AI-generated image. The images get circulated, and the negative consequences are immense. There are privacy, safety, and trust issues at play here. Students' emotional and mental health can be at stake, and worse yet, there is the threat of suicide. Students are not the only target. Teachers also have been attacked. The question remains about the role of the school in these incidents, even if there are codes of conduct.

Consider the following examples. Laguna Beach High School (CA) experienced deepfakes of students (Gonzalez, 2024; Ritchie, 2024) with nude pictures posted. The Capistrano Unified School District (CA) reported an incident in a middle school that involved an 8th-grade girl whose pictures were modified and posted by a boy (Cain & Darwish, 2024). Other incidents occurred at a high school in Illinois, a middle school in Florida, and a middle school in Beverly Hills, CA (Schermele, 2024). And there are many more. Some arrests have been made, but many educators are unclear about their roles and responsibilities when students are involved.

A slightly different scenario emerged in Malvern, PA where the target of the deepfakes was teachers, not just students (Singer, 2024). Some middle school students created and posted deepfake images of teachers in uncompromising positions. The students used imposter TikTok accounts. Teachers were smeared and their reputations attacked. The concern in this example is whether the district can do anything against the unethical behavior of the students. Can the students be held accountable? Are there legal ramifications? Can disciplinary actions be taken? What are the best courses of action that can be taken here? Some schools and districts have no grounding. Holding an assembly on responsible technology use, as Malvern did, seems weak at best. This issue will continue to be a problem in education with horrible consequences that are already happening, such as mental health issues and suicide.

Issues Concerning the Model and Framework for AI Use

There are many issues that have particular relevance to data ethics applied to the use of AI applications. These are topics that pertain to data use in general but have emerged as particularly impactful for how data use plays out in technologies that employ AI. Before exploring the issues, it is helpful to present the components of a framework for ethics in learning analytics put forth by Alwahaby and Cukurova (2024). This framework helps to think about the important components that undergird the technologies, if used appropriately. The authors identified nine unifying themes in their research:

- The need for an ethical framework—having a framework will help developers and users recognize the important components needed for ethical use;
- Privacy, surveillance, and intrusiveness issues—bringing awareness to and actions against violations that can negatively impact users;
- student agency—providing students with a level of control over their learning experiences and the ownership of their data;
- trustworthiness—considering the veracity or validity of the decisions that result from the analytics produced by the technology;
- Fairness and bias—ensuring the extent to which the underlying samples are sufficiently sensitive to a broad range of users and their characteristics and backgrounds;
- transparency and explainability—being clear about and disclosing what data is being used and the analytic process;
- accountability—ensuring that educational agencies are held accountable for inappropriate uses of data;
- awareness of the benefits and risks—understanding and weighing the challenges and opportunities involved in using learning analytics; and
- The ethics of not using the technology—determining what are the potential benefits that might be lost if educators were to not use the advanced technologies to enhance teaching and learning.

The first and perhaps the most pressing issue raised is algorithmic bias. The algorithms that underlie AI programming controls what data is used, the analytics, and how decisions are made. Thus, there are questions about the validity of the data (Kovanovic et al., 2024). According to Holmes (2023), algorithms often reflect biases and amplify them, ultimately leading to harms. Alwahaby and Cukurova (2024) note: "AI may be causing inequalities and injustices because of the sociocultural biases reflected in the data used, which could also make those AI models unfair"

(p. 40). Further, the algorithms tend to have a narrow understanding of learning (Williamson et al., 2024), and the datasets used are not neutral, sometimes reflecting particular political and social perspectives (Nguyen, 2024), both of which have consequences for decision-making. Potentially the data representations and classifications are skewed and biased. The models need to consider the context and the complexity of the decision-making process.

AI models have been criticized for having a narrow focus. They take a reductionist approach to data. This means that the models focus on specific skills, and the outcomes become mechanistic, technocratic, and superficial (Holmes, 2023; Williamson et al., 2024). The models fail to consider that not every key variable or construct can be quantified and sometimes ignore the complexity presented by students, not taking a whole child perspective. The guiding principles here are that more data is often not better and that data cannot provide a comprehensive depiction of reality (NFES, 2010).

There are technical issues at play as well. The first is data quality. No dataset is perfect and complete, and many will contain bias because they fail to adequately represent all students. Fundamental measurement principles need to be considered. The data must be accurate, representative, complete, timely, and relevant. Perhaps most importantly, the datasets must be representative of the population in question to avoid possible bias and discrimination. The data should be verifiable against human judgment. The data must be aligned to the purpose of the decision. This is about the reliability and validity of the data and the decision-making process. The data analytics must be trustworthy and reasonable. Educators must recognize that the analytics used in the AI models may contain potential bias and that the probabilistic reasoning can be wrong (NFES, 2025).

These issues are all are part of the underlying components of the data ethics framework presented in the prior chapter. Transparency is especially important because the technology can hide many of the processes. Users must be able to understand what the application is doing and how it performs. It is about interpretability. The data, the analytics, and the statistical modeling must be clear, defined, and explainable so that the data and analytics can be aligned to the intended outcomes. This means explaining how the data are collected, stored, and processed (Chaudhry et al., 2022). Given the potential technical problems, without transparency, the possible flaws cannot be remediated (NFES, 2025). Turning to the other side of the data ethics framework, it is essential for users to understand the possible risks, consider the unintended consequences of the AI models, and consider both the positive and negative outcomes. This will serve to increase trust and decrease potential harm.

Issues Pertaining to the Decision-Making Process

Decisions are the ultimate objective of the process of using data. The decisions must be based on quality data and sound analytics. The American Statistical Association's (2022) ethical guidelines document clearly lays out the appropriate actions, methods, and procedures. Yet there are limitations and concerns. Khodaei and colleagues (2024) note: "There are many risks of incorrect assumptions based on data that might lead to incorrect knowledge and decisions" (p. 1). Further, Williamson and colleagues (2024) actually warn that AI technologies "obscure" decision-making (p. 3). Data are important and essential, but an overemphasis and overreliance on data can be problematic. There needs to be human input as well, that is, human agency. Human decision-making cannot be replaced. Educators must be a key part in the pedagogical process, not just a bystander allowing the AI to take over. AI does not know everything about the needed pedagogy. However, there must be a balance. Too much data and too many analytics can be problematic, yet too much emotion can lead to impulsive decision-making (Wang, 2019).

Other Issues

There are several other issues that have potential ethical impacts from the use of AI-based technologies. A first, which has been alluded to above, is equity. There can be discrimination that results from the algorithms, the datasets, the analytics, and the interpretations. The algorithms clearly present problems in terms of their cultural sensitivity and not taking into consideration students' backgrounds, contexts, and cultural assets. In fact, the AI models often assume a deficit model and ignore diversity among students. Discrimination can include not only ethnicity and race but also disability and neurodiversity. Stereotypes can be perpetuated. There can be bias in labeling students at risk. Assumptions can be made and confirmation bias applied. As Martin (2022a) notes, although decisions may be legal, but they may not be fair.

Another set of issues focuses on the overreliance on data where data privacy, data security, and surveillance occur. These are very real concerns and can create major ethical issues. Violations of FERPA must be taken seriously. Surveillance creates a culture where there is a lack of trust. Further, there can be exploitation based on the use of data for non-educational purposes. For example, Holmes (2023) raises the issue of commercialism. This means that the vendors or developers who have access to the student data may profit in some way by the selling of the data for non-educational purposes. It is therefore essential to create a culture of transparency and accountability (Holmes, 2023; NFES, 2025) where there is mitigation of potential harms (Cohen, 2022).

Concluding Thoughts

This chapter has reviewed a number of AI-based technologies and has raised many ethical issues. Seemingly, the challenges outweigh the opportunities. Some issues are cautionary, and others are very real concerns. Many of the issues pertain to bias and discrimination. Some of the issues are technical, whereas others are based on use. Developers are working to mitigate the flaws. Make no mistake, technologies, and especially those based on AI, will continue to proliferate. Their sophistication will improve. Educators' sophistication, awareness, and literacy need to do likewise. As improvement occurs, the balance between the challenges and opportunities will shift and become more equal. That is a lofty goal toward which to strive. AI-based technologies should never replace educators. They can and should be used to supplement and enhance what educators do. Human agency will always be essential. So there are a number of balances to be put in place. For me, the grounding should be about effective and ethical data use. Effective data use is one thing. Ethical data use must go hand in hand. Responsible data use is a precept for effective data use.

4

A User's Guide to the Scenarios

Chapter Outline

Structure of the Scenarios	40
Alignment to the Codes and Standards	42
A General Statement About the Scenarios	50
Guidance for the Scenarios	51

The next two chapters present a variety of scenarios that have been written to depict authentic situations that educators may encounter. The scenarios focus on different levels of the education system and different participants. Some focus on classrooms, schools, and districts; others emphasize the role of teachers, building leaders, central administrators, and other educational staff. The impetus for the scenarios comes from various sources. The idea to use scenarios to highlight issues around data ethics follows from work I have done on data privacy, where such scenarios illustrated the complexities of challenging situations and regulations surrounding the protection of student data (Mandinach et al., 2021, 2023a, 2023b). The use of scenarios translated from my prior exploration around culturally responsive data literacy (Mandinach, 2025) and is aligned with the case studies used by Gorski and Pothini (2018) for social justice.

For these scenarios, I draw from the *MCEE* (National Association of State Technology Directors of Teacher Education and Certification (NASDTEC), 2023) and the National Education Association's (NEA) (n.d.) code of ethics to focus on key topics that professional organizations have included in their treatment of educators' ethics that can be related to data use. State standards and other regulations are also considered. Other scenarios are based on situations that have been reported by educators or observed by researchers. Yet another source is the public media; that is, educational events fraught with ethical issues that have appeared in newspapers, news reports, or other venues. The topics are obviously diverse.

Structure of the Scenarios

The intent of the scenarios is to make them as user-friendly as possible. They can be used by university professors, in-service providers, or individuals. Each scenario adheres to a common structure.

Learning Objectives

Each scenario opens with specific topical and skill-based goals that the situation addresses. The objectives are linked to data literacy skills and aspects of data ethics.

Scenario

This section lays out the situation and provides context around an event, issue, or situation that requires an understanding of the appropriate use of data.

Discussion Questions

The section provides some rudimentary questions that should structure thoughts about where data ethics may come into play. The instructor can pose the questions in class or to the in-service group or use the questions as part of an assignment.

Probing Questions

These questions are intended to require a deeper dive and more extensive consideration of the situation. They can be used for classroom discussion, online chats, essays, or other activities that require a more nuanced understanding of the scenario and data ethics. There may be no right or wrong answer here.

Discussion of the Ethical Considerations

This section can help guide users to understand some of the varying perspectives around ethics that are generated by the scenario. The section links the considerations to codes of ethics such as the *MCEE*. The section also examines various professional organizations and state standards as they pertain to data ethics. The section may also refer to relevant research.

References

Where possible, references from journal articles, whether research-based or practitioner-oriented, will be provided. The section will include references to guides and manuals where possible. It will also include articles that have appeared in the public media, such as in newspapers, blogs, and other similar sources. These are important sources because all too often, challenging ethical issues appear in social and public media before they have been addressed in research or educational policy.

When one considers ethics, and data ethics more specifically, one tends to think about the negatives, the negative impacts, consequences, and harms. One thinks about ethics violations. Many of the scenarios indeed deal with blatant infractions, and some are more nuanced. Yet, there are also positives. There are scenarios that illustrate positive ethical actions and decisions. This hopefully provides a balance and somewhat of a reality check that there are both ethical and unethical actions in terms of data use.

Alignment to the Codes and Standards

As you will see in the presentation of the scenarios, the codes and standards that are highlighted below underlie the depictions in each of the situations. Some of the particular standards will be obvious, whereas others will be more subtle. Some are more related to ethical behavior more generally construed, whereas others fall squarely on data use. The intersection of ethics and data use is sometimes tricky, but almost all educational practice is or should be grounded in data use, so the pairing is natural.

From the NEA

The NEA (n.d.) produced a governance document entitled *Code of Ethics for Educators*, which contains two overarching principles (commitment to the student and commitment to the profession). I extract here, the topics that are most relevant to data ethics. However, none of the points directly mention data, which is telling in and of itself. They are about ethical practice more generally interpreted. They all fall under Principle I and are five of eight precepts (pp. 3–4).

- Shall not unreasonably restrain the student from independent action in the pursuit of learning.
- Shall not unreasonably deny the student's access to varying points of view.
- Shall not intentionally expose the student to embarrassment or disparagement.
- Shall not, on the basis of race, color, creed, sex, national origin, marital status, political or religious beliefs, family, social, or cultural background, or sexual orientation, unfairly
  - Exclude any student from participation in any program.
  - Deny benefits to any student.
  - Grant any advantage to any student.
- Shall not discuss information about students obtained in the course of professional service unless disclosure serves a compelling professional purpose or is required by law.

Note that only the last bullet addresses data use.

From the NASDTEC

The most recent version of the *MCEE* (NASDTEC, 2023) contains thirty-eight standards relevant to data ethics. Additionally, the *MCEE* provides four definitions that relate to data ethics: harm, risk, sensitive information, and transparency. Harm is defined as "any potential action that may impair the physical, emotional, psychological, sexual, or intellectual safety and well-being of a student or a member of the school community" (p. 8). Risk is defined as "A non-desirable consequence that may occur as a result of the situation (e.g., risk to student(s), educator, colleagues, school, profession)" (p. 9). Sensitive information is defined as "information gathered through one's professional practice that, if shared, could cause harm" (p. 9). Transparency is defined as "an educator's openness with respect to one's behaviors, actions, and communications" (p. 9).

The *MCEE* contains five principles with many components and subcomponents. The principles are as follows: Responsibility to the Profession; Responsibility for Professional Competence; Responsibility to Students; Responsibility to the School Community; and Responsible and Ethical Use of Technology. Of the 38 relevant topics, none fall under Principle I; 8 under Principle II; 10 under Principle III; 8 under Principle IV; and 12 under Principle V (pp. 2–7).

- II.A.1. Using the *MCEE* and other ethics codes unique to one's discipline to guide and frame educational decision-making.
- II.A.3. Advocating for equitable educational opportunities for all students.
- II.B.2. Using appropriate assessments for the purposes for which they are intended and for which they have been validated to guide educational decisions.
- II.B.4. Seeking and using evidence, instructional data, research, and professional knowledge to inform practice.
- II.B.5. Creating, maintaining, disseminating, storing, retaining, and disposing of records and data related to one's research and practice, in accordance with, but not limited to, official guidance, policy, and laws.
- II.B.6. Using data, data sources, or findings accurately, reliably, and ethically.

- II.C.1. Increasing students' access to the curriculum, activities, and resources in order to provide a quality and equitable educational experience.
- II.C.3. Protecting students from any practice that harms or has the reasonable potential to harm.
- III.A.1. Respecting students by taking into account their individual characteristics, including but not limited to age, gender, culture, setting, ability, and socioeconomic context.
- III.A.2. Interacting with students with transparency and in appropriate settings.
- III.A.3. Communicating with students in a clear, respectful, and culturally sensitive manner.
- III.A.4. Taking into account how appearance and dress can affect one's interactions and relationships with students.
- III.B.1. Seeking to understand students' educational, academic, personal, and social needs, as well as their values, beliefs, and cultural background.
- III.B.2. Respecting the dignity, worth, and uniqueness of each, individual student, including but not limited to actual and perceived gender, gender expression, gender identify, sexual orientation, civil status, family status, religion, age, disability, race, ethnicity, socioeconomic context, and culture.
- III.B.3. Establishing and maintaining an environment that promotes the emotional, intellectual, physical, and sexual safety of all students.
- III.C.1. Respecting the privacy of students and the need to hold in confidence certain forms of student communication, documents, or information obtained in the course of professional practice.
- III.C.2. Upholding parents/guardians' legal rights, as well as any legal requirements, to reveal information related to legitimate concerns for the well-being of a student.
- III.C.3. Protecting the confidentiality of student records and releasing personal data in accordance with prescribed state and federal law and local policies.
- IV.A.1. Communicating with parents/guardians in a timely, respectful, and culturally sensitive manner that represents the students' best interests.
- IV.A.2. Demonstrating a commitment to equality, equity, diversity, and inclusion with parents/guardians.

- IV.A.4. Maintaining appropriate confidentiality with respect to student information disclosed by or to parents/guardians unless required by law.
- IV.B.2. Resolving conflicts, whenever possible, privately and respectfully and in accordance with policy.
- IV.B.3. Working to ensure a workplace environment that is free from harassment.
- IV.B.5. Keeping student safety, education, and health paramount by maintaining and sharing educational records appropriately and objectively in accordance with local policies and state and federal laws.
- IV.C.1. Maintaining the highest professional standards of accuracy, honesty, and appropriate disclosure of information when representing the school or district within the community and in public communications.
- IV.E.4. Ensuring professional responsibilities to paraprofessionals, student teachers, or interns do not interfere with responsibilities to students and their learning and well-being.
- V.A.1. Using social media transparently and primarily for purposes of teaching and learning per school and district policy. The professional educator considers the ramifications of using social media and direct communication via technology in one's interactions with students, colleagues, and the general public.
- V.A.3. Evaluating information obtained electronically for reliability and bias.
- V.A.6. Recognizing that some electronic communications are recorded under the Freedom of Information Act (FOIA) and state public access laws.
- V.A.7. Considering the implications of sharing legally protected or other sensitive information electronically, either via professional or personal devices/accounts.
- V.B.1. Being vigilant in identifying, addressing, and reporting (when appropriate and in accordance with local school, district, state, and federal policy) inappropriate and illegal materials/images in electronic or other forms.
- V.B.2. Respecting the privacy of students' presence on social media unless there is a possible risk of harm to the students or others.

- V.B.3. Being attentive to (and appropriately reporting) information concerning possible cyberbullying incidents and their potential impact on the student learning environment.
- V.C.1. Taking appropriate and reasonable measures to maintain the confidentiality of privileged information and stored or transmitted educational records.
- V.C.2. Understanding the intent of the Family Educational Rights to Privacy Act (FERPA) and how it applies to sharing student record electronically.
- V.C.3. Ensuring the rights of third parties, including the right to privacy, are not violated via the use of technology.
- V.C.4. Protecting information from being shared with unintended third parties through technology.
- V.D.1. Advocating for equal and equitable access to technology for all students.

What is interesting about the *MCEE* is that prior to the latest version in 2023, there was very little, if any, coverage of ethics around data use. It is striking that the 2023 is so comprehensive and explicit around topics that relate to data use. A final observation is that underlying these topics are diverse data sources, data that may be moment-to-moment, observed, collected, quantitative, or qualitative.

From the InTASC Standards

The *Model Core Teaching Standards and Learning Progressions* (CCSSO, 2013) lay out ten standards that are deemed essential for effective teaching. For each of the ten standards, there are also are identified performance, essential knowledge, and dispositions. A review of the InTASC Standards (Mandinach et al., 2015) yielded many specific points that are related to data literacy, particularly those that appear in Standard 6, Assessment. States that have adopted the Standards, by default, address data literacy. And an increasing number of states over the past decade have been adopting the InTASC standards (Mandinach, 2025; Mandinach et al., 2017; Mandinach et al., 2015).

There are a number of performances, essential knowledge, and dispositions relevant to data ethics in Standard 1—Learner Development; Standard 2—Learning Differences; Standard 4—Content Knowledge;

Standard 7—Planning for Instruction; and Standard 8—Instructional Strategies. Standard 9 is the one most relevant to data ethics—Professional Learning and Ethical Practice. There are three performances, three essential pieces of knowledge, and three critical dispositions worth noting here.

- 9(c) Independently and in collaboration with colleagues, the teacher uses a variety of data (e.g., systematic observation, information about learners, research) to evaluate the outcomes of teaching and learning and to adapt planning and practice.
- 9(e) The teacher reflects on his or her personal biases and accesses resources to deepen his/her own understanding of cultural, ethnic, gender, and learning differences to build stronger relationships and create more relevant learning experiences.
- 9(f) The teacher advocates models, and teaches safe, legal, and ethical use of information and technology including appropriate documentation of sources and respect for others in the use of social media.
- 9(h) The teacher knows how to use learner data to analyze practice and differentiate instruction accordingly.
- 9(i) The teacher understands how personal identity, worldview, and prior experiences affect perceptions and expectations, and recognizes how they may bias behaviors and interactions with others.
- 9(j) The teacher understands laws related to learners' rights and teacher responsibilities (e.g., educational equity, appropriate education for learners with disabilities, confidentiality, privacy, appropriate treatment of learners, and reporting in situations related to possible child abuse).
- 9(l) The teacher takes responsibility for student learning and uses ongoing analysis and reflection to improve planning and practice.
- 9(m) The teacher is committed to deepening understanding of his or her own frames of reference (e.g., culture, gender, language, abilities, ways of knowing), the potential biases in these frames, and their impact on expectations and relationships with learners and their families.
- 9(o) The teacher understands the expectations of the profession, including codes of ethics, professional standards of practice, and relevant law, and policy. (p. 41)

From the Associations for Leaders

The AASA (2007) published a code of ethics with twelve points for superintendents. None of them directly or even indirectly address data ethics. The closest in relevance is the first, where it mentions that decision-making must be based on the well-being of students.

The National Association of Secondary School Principals (n.d.) has a statement about ethics that contains ten points. Similarly, the first point also notes decision-making for student well-being. There is also another point that focuses on honesty and integrity.

The National Policy Board for Educational Administration's (2015) standards fail to mention data in the document. However, Standard 2 is "Ethics and Professional Norms" in which there are eight points, most of which address issues around bias, equity, cultural responsiveness, and an understanding of students' backgrounds and context. Given that equity is a focus of data ethics, one can extrapolate indirectly about the need for data to address these issues, but data ethics are not addressed directly.

From the National Center for Educational Statistics

The National Forum on Educational Statistics is part of the IES that focuses on data use at the state and local levels. The Forum provides guides written mostly by state and local educators that specialize in relevant aspects of data use. The *Forum Guide to Data Ethics* (NFES, 2010) provides nine canons that are key guidelines for the ethical use of data. Canons 1 through 5 are about integrity, 6 and 7 about data quality, and 8 and 9 about security.

Canon 1: Demonstrate honesty, integrity, and professionalism at all times.
Canon 2: Appreciate that, while data may represent attributes of real people, they do not describe the whole person.
Canon 3: Be aware of applicable statutes, regulations, practices, and ethical standards governing data collection and reporting.
Canon 4: Report information accurately and without bias.
Canon 5: Be accountable and hold others accountable for ethical use of data.

Canon 6: Promote data quality by adhering to best practices and operating standards.
Canon 7: Provide all relevant data, definitions, and documentation to promote comprehensive understanding and accurate analysis when releasing information.
Canon 8: Treat data systems as valuable organizational assets.
Canon 9: Safeguard sensitive data to guarantee privacy and confidentiality.
(p. 7)

NCES has produced a number of Forum Guides that are relevant to data ethics. Many are referenced throughout this volume. I encourage readers to check out the Forum website for these valuable resources (see https://nces.ed.gov/forum/publications.asp).

From State Education Agencies

Another source of guidance around data ethics can be found among documents released by state education agencies, particularly their codes of ethics. Other relevant documents might be their licensure or certification requirements. A search of the documents yielded interesting findings for the fifty states and the District of Columbia. While six states have nothing that relates to data ethics, several states defer to the *MCEE*, which now contains significant coverage as noted above.

Many of the codes focused on a few general topics, such as confidentiality, testing and test security, technology, and integrity (not always around data use). For example, twenty-four states mentioned confidentiality, five privacy, two FOIA, and three FERPA. For testing and assessment issues, four states noted test security, three mentioned assessments, and three addressed assessment literacy, perhaps not using that terminology. Relatedly, four states discussed using multiple measures and five diverse data sources, both key tenets of assessment literacy and data literacy. Technology is emerging as an ethical topic with six states mentioning the limitations of technology, six concerns about social media, one about cyberbullying, and one about inappropriate digital images. Issues around honesty, integrity, and trust (ten states), truthfulness (two states), and equity (five states) were considered. Five codes mentioned using data, five facts, and five evidence. Six states mentioned falsification, one disclosure, two misrepresentation, three accuracy, and six distortion or suppression.

Habits of mind or dispositions of data literacy also came into play, with five states noting the use of data to inform practice, four to address student well-being, and two about the belief that all students can learn. Other topics included do no harm (three states), being a mandated reporter (one state, addressing bias (one state), fairness (one state, and communication (two states).

There are states that actually have specific principles that focus on either data or ethics, but they never definitively address the intersection of the two concepts. That said, there are a few states that are quite explicit about how data should be used appropriately to address student needs and inform practice. For example, Delaware talks about using evidence to adapt practice to student needs. Maryland and Maine are clear about the need for transparency in their decision-making. Maine also specifies the need to use data and evidence accurately and reliably. North Dakota notes the importance to not misrepresent information. Utah discusses the need to use facts for formulate actions. Both Hawaii and Michigan clearly state the need to use evidence and instructional data to inform practice and to understand students' cultures and backgrounds to meet their needs.

Clearly, the state education agencies address more about professionalism than data ethics in their codes of ethics. This does not come as a surprise when one considers that NASDTEC only integrated data ethics into the *MCEE* in 2023. There is a real need to address the topic as more educators are confronted with challenges around data, particularly from various technologies.

A General Statement About the Scenarios

In my prior book on culturally responsive data literacy (Mandinach, 2025), I made it a point not to not use names of people, schools, and districts from which ethnicity, race, and religion could be inferred. This is to avoid any possible stereotyping and assumptions. Names included in the scenarios are meant to be neutral. To achieve that goal, I again use the names of my friends' colleagues', and tennis teammates' pets. It is also a fun thing to do, to put in print their fur babies. The names may refer to students, educators, parents, schools, and districts. I have also tried to balance gender in a way that there is equality in the number of male and female administrators and teachers to avoid stereotypes there. Similarly, there is a balance between successful and challenged students.

Another caveat about the scenarios is that they are meant to be edgy, often to make users feel uncomfortable as they experience the situation. The intent is not to offend but to stimulate critical thought about the ethical dilemmas and potentially controversial situations. One can question if there is a right or wrong response to the scenarios. There will be plenty of gray areas left to interpretation. And that is fine, but at the very least, the ambiguity should motivate discussion around the various ways the scenarios can play out. For some scenarios, I leave the outcomes and interpretations completely open for interpretation.

A final caveat is that while some scenarios may be situated within a content area or grade level, the expectation is that the foundational concepts can be generalized. Certainly, some topics must be specific to an age group or content-specific, simply by the nature of the situation.

It is my hope that users can extract the scenarios most relevant to their own experiences and learn from how the situation is explained. I do not provide definitive answers. That is left to the users, the professors, and the in-service providers to fill in the blanks from their practice and policies. There might be nuances and variations across settings and states in terms of regulations, laws, and policies. The objective here is to raise many questions about ethical dilemmas related to data use that educators may face and consider some of the implications in terms of potential harms, intended and unintended consequences, and effects on educational practice.

Guidance for the Scenarios

As you work through the scenarios, it is important for you to keep in mind the theoretical grounding laid out in Chapter 2. Transparency and consequences are foundational in all of the scenarios. Consider in each instance whether the educators are being transparent about how they are using and analyzing the data and whether the conclusions drawn, interpretations made, and actionable steps are valid and reasonable.

Also, consider whether the educators have considered the intended and unintended consequences and if there might be potential harms that result from the decisions. So ask yourself:

- Is there transparency in the decision-making process?
- Did the educators fully consider the consequences of the decision?

Transparency and consequences are the two main components of the theoretical framework, but the four interacting factors also require consideration. These are the technical, social, political, and philosophical factors. Questions to consider here might include the following:

- Did the educators use the appropriate data and analytics based on the decision to be made? This speaks to validity and reliability and the other technical aspects of decision-making.
- Did the educators consider the social issues surrounding the decision, including equity?
- Did the educators show evidence of a particular philosophical perspective that might have influenced the decision-making process? For example, is there a belief that all students can learn?
- Is there evidence of political pressure that has influenced the decision-making process? In particular, is there evidence that accountability may have impacted the process?

5
First Set of Scenarios

Chapter Outline

Banned Books	54
Scary Reading Material	57
Balancing the Teaching of Historic Events	60
Assumptions Versus Data	65
Cameras	67
Facial Recognition	69
Deepfake	71
Denial	74
Bullying	78
Teaching Art History	81
Sanewashing	84
Science Isn't About Beliefs	87
Classroom Monitoring	89
Electronic Essay Scoring	92
Data Dashboards	94
Disclosed or Undisclosed Heath Issue	97
Pronouns	99
Underlying App Data	101
Accountability	104
Student Newspaper	107
Support Services	109
Surveys	111
Online Threat	114

The scenarios contained in this chapter and the following chapter are varied. Some scenarios directly address topics found in the codes of ethics, whereas others are drawn from practice and issues covered in research and the media.

The following scenarios are contained in this chapter:

Banned Books
Scary Reading Material
Balancing the Teaching of Historic Events
Assumptions Versus Data
Cameras
Facial Recognition
Deepfake
Denial
Bullying
Teaching Art History
Sanewashing
Science Isn't About Beliefs
Classroom Monitoring
Electronic Essay Scoring
Data Dashboards
Disclosed or Undisclosed Medical Issue
Pronouns
Underlying App Data
Accountability
Student Newspaper
Support Services
Surveys
Online Threat

Banned Books

Learning Objectives

- Understand the need to have multiple data points from which to make reliable decisions.

- Understand the potential harm that can result from external pressures.
- Consider the balance between policy and practice.

Scenario

Mr. Enzo is a teacher at Fonzie High School. He teaches literature to juniors and seniors. He covers books that are considered the "classics," those that have been in the curriculum for years, as well as including recent books that he feels might be more relevant, timely, and of interest to his students. Mr. Enzo has been very deliberate and cautious in his selections, being aware that some books may trigger reactions from certain students, as his classes are diverse.

One of the classes has been reading a particular book that Mr. Enzo has used for years. He has never had any issues or complaints about this book. The students seem really engaged in the content and have been having lively discussions. Mr. Enzo sensed that they looked forward to more discussion and writing about the book. Mr. Enzo gets a message from the office that he should stop by at the end of the school day. Ms. Ivy, the principal, is in her office with the visibly agitated parents of one of her students. Mr. Remi explains that his son came home a few days ago and described the recent book and the ensuing discussions. Mr. Remi did not like what he heard and was concerned about the appropriateness of the book. He is demanding that the book be removed from the curricula. To Mr. Enzo, it is unclear if Mr. Remi understands the instructional objectives of the book or even if he has read the book to be able to make an objective decision about the content. Seemingly, his objections are based on his interpretations of his son's reporting.

Discussion Questions

- What do you think of this situation?
- What should Ms. Ivy do?
- What should Mr. Enzo do?
- What rights does Mr. Remi have in demanding that a book be removed from the curriculum?

Probing Questions

- Discuss whether a single data point, in this case, one parent, can require an action such as banning a book.
- Discuss the actions Ms. Ivy and Mr. Enzo should take in this case, especially if there were several concerned parents, not just one individual.
- Discuss the concept of book banning in general.
- Discuss how choices of books are made and whether it makes a difference if the book in question is a "classic" or a more recent choice.
- Discuss the issue of validity and reliability of having one student's comments impact what is taught and what should be removed.
- Discuss whether you think Mr. Remi has a legitimate case for removal.

Discussion of the Ethical Considerations

Book banning has become a very real challenge in education. It is highly contentious. Books can be banned because they contain pornographic material or because they are simply deemed unsuitable for a certain age group. Books can be banned because the individual fails to take into consideration the context of the information. However, books that do not fall into these categories are still being removed, including classics that have been taught for many years. There is even a website, BookLooks.org, that provides guidance for getting books banned. Books are rated on a scale of 1 to 5, with 5 being the most offensive. Grounds for banning include sexual content, drugs, molestation, and "alternative" sexual identities and ideologies.

Litigation is in process on the basis of First Amendment rights. Policies in some states and districts have made national news and have raised significant concerns about the rights of individuals to remove valued resources from curricula. In 2023, one mother in Florida requested that over eighty books be removed, not just from the curricula, but also from the library. The form the individual filled out for each book asked if the requester had read the "offending" book. In each case, the mother had not read a single one of the books. One can walk into large bookstore chains in some locations and find a table of banned books prominently displayed. The reasons for book banning do not have to be logical. Oftentimes, there is no rational reason given. Educators, authors, and publishers maintain such actions are tantamount to censorship under the guise of protecting the children. This is a conundrum for educators. Policy mandated by politicians may overrule sound educational practice. One must question how educators should respond. If every parent has a say in what is to be taught or not, eventually there will be nothing left in the curricula that is deemed acceptable, if all it takes is one parent to be offended by a particular book. A related concern is that almost any statement made by an educator could potentially offend someone, making them hesitant to say anything, certainly nothing controversial. What happens if a student goes home and misrepresents a discussion or incident in the classroom? Who can come to the support of the educators?

References

Hardle, A. (2025, February 14). Scottsdale Unified schools remove, restrict books after conservative challenge. *Arizona Republic.* https://www.azcentral.com/story/news/local/scottsdale-education/2025/02/14/scottsdale-unified-schools-remove-books-from-libraries/78259111007/

Nguyen, T. (2024, September 29). Schools, libraries see rise in book bans. *Arizona Republic.* https://arizonarepublic-az.newsmemory.com/?token=c0a1d82db4735172039b90deb67734a1&cnum=7646d942-26d2-e711-b65f-90b11c343abd&fod=1111111-0&selDate=20240930&licenseType=paid_subscriber&

Ritter, M. E. (2024, September 3). Suit targets book bans in Fla. schools. *Arizona Republic.* https://arizonarepublic-az.newsmemory.com/?token=c2d14cf4616c4e25fb9891a29a0da9d3&cnum=7646d942-26d2-e711-b65f-90b11c343abd&fod=1111111-0&selDate=20240903&licenseType=paid_subscriber&

Scary Reading Material

Learning Objectives

- Understand the actions and rights of parents.
- Navigate divergent perspectives.

- Triangulate data points.
- Consider the consequences of a decision.

Scenario

Ms. Lily is the mother of Riley, an incoming eighth grader. During the summer, Riley's school, Moose Middle School, requires students to work through a number of books in preparation for the school year. The reading list includes *The Scarlet Letter* and *Frankenstein*, among others. Ms. Lily is keen on the idea of having Riley read these books. She enjoyed them when she was a student. And Riley is a diligent student who dives into the reading list.

At back-to-school night, Ms. Lily noticed an unusual number of parents gathered at Moose. They are engaged in an animated or even heated discussion. Ms. Lily hears the outgrowth of the discussion when Mr. Otis calls the classroom to order. Immediately some of the parents begin attacking Mr. Otis about the reading list, saying that some of the books, like *Frankenstein*, are just too scary for children of this age, and have refused to let their children read such material. Ms. Lily is shocked at the tone of the discussion. She and Riley had some great discussions about the book during the summer, and he obviously liked it.

Mr. Otis tries to engage the angry parents, but to no avail. He maintains the book has been taught for years. It is part of the accepted curriculum. Mr. Otis stops short of saying that students who have not done the summer reading will be penalized. The parents threaten to take their complaints to higher levels, like the superintendent or the school board.

Discussion Questions

- How should Mr. Otis handle this situation?
- With whom should Mr. Otis consult?
- Should Ms. Lily weigh in on the discussion, providing an opposing perspective?

Probing Questions

- Discuss whether parents should be able to mandate what is taught or not?

- Discuss what actions parents should take if such a book is removed yet it is an approved part of the curriculum and has significant educational value.
- Discuss who the right decision-makers here, as Mr. Otis does not have control over the curriculum, other educators do.
- Discuss what accommodations Ms. Otis should make for the students whose parents object to the material.
- Consider if Ms. Otis should provide alternative readings for the students where the book is deemed inappropriate.
- Discuss whether Mr. Otis has the right to penalize students who have not done the reading.
- Discuss whether the questionable book(s) have been acceptable and taught for years without complaints or incidents.

Discussion of the Ethical Considerations

We currently live in a society where people are hypersensitive about many things, rightly or wrongly. Certain books, names, or events are fine for some people but may offend or trigger others. Everyone has their own perspective, given their context, background, and sensitivities. It is important for educators to take into consideration differing points of view and be amenable to open discussions. But one has to question if there is a limit. Being cautious and sensitive to differing perspectives is good. Showing empathy is good. But how much is too much in terms of accommodating or acquiescing to every divergent perspective? It is doubtful there can ever be complete consensus. In this case, parents who are proponents of a questioned book may opt to work with their child outside of the classroom. But not all parents are able to do that. Parents who object to a book may refuse to have their child participate. It is a conundrum for educators. Someone is surely going to object to something, and can that one individual determine what is taught or not?

There also may be an issue about which parents are making the demands. Let me recount a relevant conversation I encountered years ago between two seasoned principals. The first principal led a middle school in an affluent community. The second principal led a high school that primarily served a lower-class, Pacific Rim immigrant population. The first principal commented that parents at his school were constantly on his back, making demands about what and how to teach, because after all, they were highly educated professionals. They threatened to pull their children out and send them to private school if the demands were not met. The principal commented that the educators were treated like au pairs or hired help, not teachers. In contrast, the second principal countered with, that his teachers were revered by the parents and treated with respect because of their experience and expertise. The parents entrusted their children to the school because they wanted what was best for the children and wanted them to learn. What were the takeaways from this encounter? Parents at both schools care deeply about their children, but the affluent and highly educated parents think they know more than the educators and behaved accordingly. Parents at the less affluent school trusted the educators as professionals. The question to consider here is to what extent should parents have a say in or even demand or control what is or is not taught? Then how should educators respond to those demands? Correspondingly, what data or research should educators use to make these decisions?

References

Finn, R. (2007, July 8). Summer reading title prompts resistance from parents, not students. *New York Times*. https://www.nytimes.com/2007/07/08/nyregion/nyregionspecial2/08colli.html

The Learning Network. (2022, February 18). What students are saying about banning books from school libraries. *New York Times*. https://www.nytimes.com/2022/02/18/learning/students-book-bans.html

Balancing the Teaching of Historic Events

Learning Objectives

- Understand the sensitivities around controversial topics and how to handle them.

- Consider how to triangulate among differing perspectives.
- Determine how to navigate delicate discussions.
- Understand potential harms and consequences.

Scenario

Mr. Huey is a senior, tenured social studies teacher at Gracie High School. Mr. Huey has been teaching for years, and he is popular with the students because he likes to infuse history with current events. He firmly believes that history is cyclical and events will recur with time. The intention here is to help the students understand that historical events do not occur in isolation; that there are many similarities across time. He uses systems thinking to make his points. For example, Mr. Huey challenges his students to consider the similarities among events like the American Revolution, the French Revolution, and the overthrow of the tsars in Russia or the shah in Iran. He wants his students to understand that history repeats itself under certain conditions and to recognize the similarities across the situations.

Mr. Huey begins a set of lessons about the rise of dictators and autocrats, focusing on events in the 20th century in Europe. He discusses the rise of Mussolini in Italy. But his primary focus is on how Hitler came to power in Germany, a topic with extensive research. He asks his students to watch *Triumph of the Will*, a 1935 propaganda film by Leni Riefenstahl. At best, this film is a chilling reminder of tyranny and compliance. He also asks his students to watch *Judgment at Nuremberg*, a 1961 fictional film that explores the culpability of judges who had to render justice during the Nazi regime. This film explores issues about the extent to which individuals will obey orders even when they may be immoral or unethical. Relevant to the films, particularly the second one, Mr. Huey discusses a classic set of psychological experiments conducted by Stanley Milgram about obedience, trying to address how seemingly innocent people can do horrible things when told to do them; the pressure to comply.

Mr. Huey asks the class to discuss the materials. The class is clearly engaged. There is lively discussion. The discussion turns to more recent events and a student, Maggie, draws a parallel to current events, and the rise of extremism. Mr. Huey tries to be very careful here because the discussion could become highly politicized and polarizing. It could evolve into some ugly stuff. He knows the class could quickly mirror the diversity and what has been happening across the country, and that is not his intention.

An Alternative to the Scenario

Mr. Huey, rather than the students, notes that the rise of Nazism is similar to current events.

A Continuation of the Scenario

Ginger, a student, goes home and reports to her parents about the reading materials, the lesson, and the discussion. The parents immediately request a meeting with the principal and superintendent. Action is taken and Mr. Huey is fired.

Discussion Questions

- Do you think Mr. Huey did anything wrong?
- Should Mr. Huey's tenure and seniority make any difference? Should he be protected?
- Does it make a difference that Mr. Huey has taught this lesson and used the resources with no prior consequences?

Probing Questions

- Discuss how Mr. Huey should have structured the lesson.
- Discuss how Mr. Huey should respond to the student who raised the parallel to current events.
- Discuss whether the actions taken by the school district were appropriate.
- Given the current polarization, how should historical events be taught so that no one is offended, but also shows the potentially impactful consequences?
- Discuss the situation and the ramifications if Mr. Huey is the one who notes the similarities between the 1930's and current events.

- Discuss the situation and the ramifications if Mr. Huey simply asks the class to discuss, and some of the students note the similarities between the 1930s and current events.
- Discuss how it may be possible to teach historical events such as Hitler's Germany without drawing parallels to other incidents in history where totalitarianism emerged, including recent events.
- Discuss how teachers should teach history in such a hypersensitive time around what may be controversial and politicized topics.

Discussion of the Ethical Considerations

Teaching social studies or history can be a challenging enterprise, in part because views of past events have changed over time. What were once accepted historical events or persons are now being reconsidered in terms of current perspectives. For example, Woodrow Wilson is now seen as a racist. Thomas Jefferson and George Washington are criticized for having been slave owners. Robert E. Lee and other Confederate generals are considered traitors to the country. Names are being removed from streets, schools, and buildings, statues taken down, and history rewritten.

Additionally, historical events are systemic. There are many similarities that can be found in events leading up to revolutions, wars, and trends. Part of teaching history is identifying and discussing those similarities. But this can be unsettling when events are controversial or even seemingly evident. Over time, there have been many bad guys—tyrants, despots, autocrats, and dictators. There is a long and established list of individuals who have created horrible atrocities against humanity in their own countries and in the attempted takeovers of those countries. Some are current, and much can be learned about the circumstances that created similar situations throughout history. The facts around the historical events typically are accepted. The current events are more controversial, depending on many things. Take, for example, perspectives on recent conflicts like the invasion of Ukraine, the situation in Gaza, or the rise of extremism that has created frightening political divides and unrest. Making any sort of intended or unintended political statement is sure to elicit strong feelings. So how can a teacher present topics around current and past historical events without offending someone?

In the above scenario, the safest approach for Mr. Huey may have been to avoid drawing any parallels between Hitler and current events. He could certainly teach about the Hitler era and let the students draw their own conclusions. He could let the students voice their own positions and even draw the apparent parallels. But for him to explicitly make a statement might be risky. Should he be fired for this is problematic? One would have to be concerned about saying anything, even the most innocent statement, that could lead to removal. It is truly a delicate situation.

A further confounding issue is what if a student goes home and complains about something that happened or was said in class and totally misconstrues it or lies about it through disinformation. How can teachers defend themselves? I bring up an interesting debate that resulted from the suggestion of installing cameras in classrooms. In 2022, Kari Lake ran for Governor of Arizona and proposed to put a camera in every classroom. This proposal created a huge controversy. Teachers were outraged. It would violate their privacy. More importantly, it would violate student privacy regulations. I had a discussion with a friend of mine in another state who has taught for many years. I was surprised by her response. She welcomed the opportunity to have a camera. The reason was salient; it made some sense. If a student went home and said that Ms. Olive had said something and totally misrepresented the comment, she would have hard evidence to rebut the inaccurate and false accusation. I sincerely hope that education has not come to the point that anything teachers say (of course within reason) can be held against them.

References

Mandinach, E. B. & Cline, H. F. (1994). *Classroom dynamics: Implementing a technology-based learning environment.* Lawrence Erlbaum Associates.

Milgram, S. (1973). The perils of obedience. *Harper's Magazine, 247*(1483), 62–77.

Milwicki, A., Carey, M. H., & Winikka-Lydon, J. (2023, April 17). "Never again" starts with education. *Learning for Justice.* https://www.learningforjustice.org/magazine/never-again-starts-with-education

Assumptions Versus Data

Learning Objectives

- Learn the importance of using data as opposed to making assumptions.
- Understand that technology can be fallible.

Scenario

The Harley School District has begun using software to detect potential plagiarism. The software company promises that the package has 99 percent accuracy. The software is being adopted in the wake of students using ChatGPT and other technologies to write their essays, papers, and assignments. Teachers have been trained to use the program, yet some are hesitant. They are old school and say they can recognize plagiarism. Ms. Leana has adopted the technology, whereas Mr. Bruce prefers to make the determination on his own.

The two teachers actually decide to conduct an experiment. Both will grade the same papers using Mr. Bruce's old school method. They will also submit the papers to the software to determine validity and reliability. Mr. Bruce makes some assumptions based on his experience. Ms. Leana sees things slightly differently. And the program yields even different results.

Discussion Questions

- Would you believe the analysis by the software or the teacher?
- What do you think of plagiarism detection software?
- What are the ramifications of making assumptions?

Probing Questions

- Discuss the issues surrounding the use of experience versus data.
- Discuss making assumptions versus using data.

- Discuss whether you think data produced by such technology can be inaccurate.
- Discuss what the outcome should be the outcome if the two teachers agree but the software results differ. Who do you believe? Or if the teachers disagree but one has the results confirmed by the software?.
- Discuss how you can make plagiarism a learning opportunity in the classroom.
- Discuss the ramifications and potential harms if a teacher falsely accuses a student of plagiarism.
- Discuss the benefits and issues of students using generative technology for their assignments.
- Discuss the implications for teachers, both the benefits and the limitations, of using technology for the detection of plagiarism.

Discussion of the Ethical Considerations

"There are many risks of incorrect assumptions based on data that might lead to incorrect knowledge and decisions" (Khodaei et al., 2024, p. 1). One of the foundational principles of responsible data use is to use data, facts, and evidence, not feelings, anecdotes, or assumptions. Assumptions are posed without proof or an evidentiary base. Responsible and effective data use must rely on the use of facts. Sound decisions must be based on evidence. However, it is important to note that interpretations made on data can be up for debate. It is not uncommon for individuals to look at the same data and potentially draw different conclusions or interpretations. Furthermore, it also is important not to diminish teachers' experience and expertise.

References

Khodaei, S., Abdelrazeq, A., & Isenhardt, I. (2024). Towards categorizing ethical questions in data literacy. *Ing.grid*. https://www.inggrid.org/article/id/3967/

Mandinach, E. B. & Gummer, E. S. (2016b). *Data literacy for educators: Making it count in teacher preparation and practice*. Teachers College Press.

Cameras

Learning Objectives

- Understand the privacy issues surrounding the use of cameras in various places throughout a school building.
- Understand the limitations of using cameras and their purposes.

Scenario

The Jackson School District has installed cameras in various places throughout its buildings to primarily deter vandalism and inappropriate behavior. For example, cameras are installed at all entrances, in the hallways, overlooking the parking lot and the athletic fields, in the office, the cafeteria, and the library, as well as a few other locations. The data can help resource officers and school administrators monitor the safety of the campuses. Students and staff are aware of the cameras, as signs are posted and visible. The district even considered installing cameras in each classroom to identify possible problems and student violence.

Yet despite the cameras, problems have been detected. The cameras have caught students smoking, doing drugs, having sex, committing violent acts against other students, committing theft, and more. The cameras are actually capturing the targeted inappropriate activities. But concerns are being raised about possible over-surveillance.

Discussion Questions

- Do you think the district has the right to install the cameras?
- Do you think the intention makes sense?

Probing Questions

- Discuss the ramifications of the cameras being used and detecting inappropriate activities.
- Discuss the student privacy implications due to the use of cameras.

- Discuss the ethical implications of having cameras installed.
- Discuss your thoughts about cameras in the classroom.
- Discuss whether you think having the posted signage makes any difference in terms of actions the students may take relating to violations and the use of the footage as evidence for handing out punishment.

Discussion of the Ethical Considerations

This scenario presents a conundrum. On one side, there are the intended and possible positive consequences—that the cameras can catch problematic behavior, vandalism, or suspicious activity that can then be addressed. Cameras may be able to identify potential safety threats. On the other side, there are the unintended and negative consequences that may cause potential harms. With cameras throughout the school, the perception of over-surveillance becomes very real. The cameras may deter bad behavior but the fact that cameras can capture almost any action can lead to anxiety, mistrust, and emotional distress, not to mention the possible misinterpretation of activities caught on camera. Take, for example, both the pros and cons of the following action. A student enters the bathroom and does not exit for an extended period of time. If someone reports the student late for class or missing, the camera footage can provide potentially valuable information. The student may have been bullied in the bathroom or may legitimately be ill and need time in there. The cameras could identify other students who were in the bathroom at the same time and use that information for questioning if an incident had occurred. The cameras could identify students who were destroying school property, fighting, or doing drugs as the scenario lays out. But there is also an intrusiveness factor at play here. Cameras have become ubiquitous in society. For example, law enforcement can use those cameras to their advantage to identify victims and track perps. Without the cameras, their jobs would be much more difficult. The cameras provide credible evidence about the location of individuals at a given point in time. Schools and districts must carefully weigh the advantages and disadvantages to the installation and use of cameras. Administrators should make clear the policies surrounding their use so that there are no misunderstandings.

Reference

Parrish, M., & Sullivan, N. (2024b, August 14). Arizona schools embrace AI, facial recognition cameras. *Arizona Republic*. https://arizonarepublic-az.newsmemory.com/?token=581ae1b5e637d4982b78341caec9fb66&cnum=7646d942-26d2-e711-b65f-90b11c343abd&fod=1111111-0&selDate=20240906&licenseType=paid_subscriber&

Facial Recognition

Learning Objectives

- Understand that the algorithms underlying facial recognition may not be able to accurately detect accurately the faces of some groups of students.
- Recognize that the data from some technologies may be inadvertently flawed and could potentially harm some students.

Scenario

The Lake School District recently installed facial recognition technology for student IDs to control the entry points and prevent the admission of intruders into the school. This was done solely for the sake of school safety. Students and educators were issued photo ID's that must be swiped to enter the buildings, and their names and times of entry get recorded. This is much like safety monitoring in hotels, where security can determine who entered a room and at what time (i.e., a housekeeper or a guest). The expectation was that the technology would help to protect the schools. A resource officer would monitor the point of entry to make sure the process goes smoothly and provide assistance if entry is rejected.

But recently, there have been incidents of the system failing to recognize students and staff who rightfully should be allowed entry. The resource officers led by Mr. Purrsephone do have lists of both students and staff in the event the technology fails or if an individual's entry is rejected. The officers take the collected lists of rejections to the administration for analysis. The analysis yields a disturbing pattern among the rejections. The system disproportionately fails to recognize faces of color. Their rejection rate is significantly higher than for Caucasian faces.

Discussion Questions

- Do you think the district should keep the facial recognition system?
- Do you think such technology has a place in schools regardless of its accuracy?

Probing Questions

- Discuss the ethics of adopting a technology that is known to potentially discriminate against some groups of students or staff.
- Discuss what you think the Lake District should do to mitigate the situation.
- Discuss how you think the data accuracy can be improved.

Discussion of the Ethical Considerations

When technology shows bias against specific subgroups of individuals, it presents a real problem. The program and its underlying algorithms may not have been tested sufficiently on diverse populations, and therefore the data driving the recognition are flawed and lack sufficient sensitivity. It is important to recognize that bias and potential harm could ensue. Those who purchase such technology must be fully aware of these limitations and the ramifications of false outcomes.

Some districts and even states have banned the technology due to risks for civil rights. For example, the New York Office of Information Technology Services (2023) decided the risks outweigh the benefits. There may be too many false positives for people of color as well as for non-binary and trans individuals. Yet some districts are adopting the technology, not only for entry points but more readily for facial recognition that leads to surveillance for school safety purposes.

References

New York Office of Information Technology Services. (2023, September 27). *State education department issues determination on biometric identifying technology in schools.* https://www.nysed.gov/news/2023/state-education-department-issues-determination-biometric-identifying-technology-schools

Parrish, M. & Sullivan, N. (2024a, August 9). AI, facial recognition security camera systems coming to Arizona schools. *Arizona Republic.* https://www.azcentral.com/story/news/local/arizona-education/2024/08/09/artificial-intelligence-facial-recognition-adopted-for-school-safety-arizona/74637433007/

Parrish, M. & Sullivan, N. (2024b, August 14). Arizona schools embrace AI, facial recognition cameras. *Arizona Republic.* https://arizonarepublic-az.newsmemory.com/?token=581ae1b5e637d4982b78341caec9fb66&cnum=7646d942-26d2-e711-b65f-90b11c343abd&fod=1111111-0&selDate=20240906&licenseType=paid_subscriber&

Yoder-Himes, D. R., Asif, A., Kinney, K., Brandt, T. J., Cecil, R. E., Himes, P. R., Cashon, C., Hopp, R. M. P., & Ross, E. (2022). Racial, skin tone, and sex disparities in automated proctoring software. *Frontiers in Education, 7,* 881449. https://doi.org/10.3389/feduc.2022.881449

Deepfake

Learning Objectives

- Understand the harm that can be caused by using deepfakes.
- Consider what responsibility school districts have when teachers or students are being attacked through the use of deepfake software.

Scenario

The Winslow School District recently made the news for all the wrong reasons. Some middle school teachers and students were being attacked through the use of deepfake software. Some students were using facial pictures of both teachers and other students and attaching lewd depictions of their bodies, some of which included sexual activity. The pictures were then distributed on social media.

Teachers and the parents of the affected students complained to school administrators. The pictures were horrible and impacted the reputations of the teachers, who complained vehemently to both administrators and union representatives. The parents also sought help from the district. They considered the incidents yet another form of cyberbullying and demanded that the district take action against the perpetrators.

Discussion Questions

- Do teachers have different rights than students in terms of how districts handle the issue?
- Is it the responsibility of the district to protect the teachers?

Probing Questions

- Discuss what rights teachers have in demanding action and protection from the school district.
- Discuss what differences there might be in protecting students versus teachers.
- Discuss the ramifications of using deepfake software to cause harm to others within and beyond school boundaries.

Discussion of the Ethical Considerations

Deepfakes are becoming pervasive as a way to distort information, recordings, images, graphics, and photos. Much of deepfake activities are done to cause harm. They are malicious. Because young people have become technologically adept, it is not uncommon for minors to wreak havoc using the technology. One only has to conduct a search and an overwhelming number of hits appear across the country.

Deepfakes are obviously inappropriate and unethical, but they may or may not be illegal. A question remains about responsibility and the role schools should take. Students and teachers are being harassed and harmed by students. It is unclear if such incidents are a district issue, a police issue, or both.

Singer (2024) recounts an incident at a middle school in Pennsylvania where students created deepfake lewd photos of teachers and posted them on social media. Teachers' reputations were impacted. Students were suspended. They said it was a joke, but it was completely malicious behavior. District officials have limited control over such behavior and what students do off-campus.

In some cases, students were arrested, police reports have been filed, some the cases dropped, and for others the students were expelled. Educators are searching for solutions as the events continue to occur with increasing frequency. Codes of ethics often exist but do little to mitigate these offenses. Educators may push for helping students to understand appropriate and responsible behavior using technology but it has not worked. As the Singer article notes, students then turned to finding workarounds to continue to post inappropriate images. Teachers' privacy has obviously been violated.

References

Cain, J. & Darwish, M. (2024, April 11). Fast rise in AI nudes of teens has schools, legal system scrambling for solutions. *Orange County Register*. https://www.ocregister.com/2024/04/11/fast-rise-in-ai-nudes-of-teens-has-unprepared-schools-legal-system-scrambling-for-solutions/

Haskins, C. (2024, March 8). Florida middle schoolers arrested for allegedly creating deepfake nudes of classmates. *Wired*. https://www.wired.com/story/florida-teens-arrested-deepfake-nudes-classmates/

Ritchie, E. I. (2024, April 2). Laguna Beach High investigating AI-generated inappropriate photos of students. *Orange County Register*. https://www.ocregister.com/2024/04/02/laguna-beach-high-investigating-ai-generated-inappropriate-photos-of-students/

Singer, N. (2024, July 6). Students target teachers in group TikTok attack, shaking their school. *New York Times*. https://www.nytimes.com/2024/07/06/technology/tiktok-fake-teachers-pennsylvania.html

Denial

Learning Objectives

- Learn how to discern fact from fiction and use evidence-based decision-making.
- Consider how to handle students who fail to accept an evidentiary base.

Scenario

Ms. Speckles is a social studies teacher at Goliath High School. She loves to engage her students in critical thinking about historical events. Mr. Pickles is a science teacher at the same school. Ms. Speckles has been preparing a unit on the Holocaust, and Mr. Pickles is doing one on climate change. Both topics have an extensive research base on which the two teachers are grounding their lessons. Ms. Speckles uses original materials, film clips, and provides links to sites such as the US Holocaust Museum and Yad Vashem in Israel. Mr. Pickles provides age-appropriate materials written by esteemed scientists, oceanographers, and climatologists.

They present the units to their classes. The students dive into the materials, or so they think. As classroom discussions commence, both teachers are confronted by some students who express concerning views. Mabel, a student in the world history class insists that the Holocaust never happened. She has looked at websites and recounts blurbs from speakers who have attended white nationalist events. She claims the genocide of 6,000,000 people is complete trash. Other students begin to present counterarguments, while others stay silent, obviously feeling uncomfortable. The class has a few Jewish students who are particularly unnerved, with family members who were either murdered or were survivors. A similar incident happens in Mr. Pickles's class. A few students do not believe in climate change and express their feeling that the science is total bunk.

Both Mr. Pickles and Ms. Speckles are unnerved by the level of intensity of the denial. They discuss the events that occurred in their classes after school in the teachers' lounge. Other teachers overhear the discussion and have said they have had similar experiences. Collectively, they try to determine how they should handle their classes tomorrow.

Discussion Questions

- Should the teachers have allowed the students to express their perspectives while denying the data and evidence?
- Should the teachers have shut down the denial?

Probing Questions

- Discuss what actions teachers should take to mitigate the espousal of conspiracy theories, denial, and falsehoods.
- Consider what might be effective instructional strategies to correct the falsehoods.
- More generally, how should teachers handle situations in which they know, based on sound data or evidence, that students are either not understanding or are purposefully spreading disinformation?

Discussion of the Ethical Considerations

Denial of evidence is a very real threat throughout society, not just in schools. Denial is much stronger than skepticism. It is about values, beliefs, ignorance, and even malfeasance. Quoting some of my prior writing (Mandinach & Gummer, 2021a):

> The rejection of science may be grounded in the desire for something to be false, a drive to denial, an effort to make something fit one's worldview, frame of reference, belief structure, or social circumstances; or about not knowing when to use evidence as opposed to intuition. (p. 19).

Certain content may be disproportionately affected by denial, particularly in history and science where there are factions who vehemently disagree with evidence around topics such as the Holocaust, climate change, smoking, vaccination policies, Covid, evolution, intelligent design, flat-world theories, and more. Some denial is based in religious beliefs, political positions, attitudes, social factors, and emotions. There is little foundation other than the rejection of evidence. The rise of not only misinformation (unintended skewing) but disinformation (intentional distortion of facts), has stimulated research and writing about how to deal with the issue.

Authors and researchers are trying to call attention to the use of falsehoods, misconceptions, and confirmation bias. Kavanaugh and Rich (2018) discuss the decay of truth by noting that facts can be verified, whereas interpretations can be debated. They use the term "blurring" to denote the lack of differentiation between opinion over facts. The authors comment that there is an increasing skepticism over evidence and lack of trust more generally in the use of data and analytics. A fascinating book by scholars at the University of Washington, entitled, *Calling Bullshit*, explores how society is being inundated by inaccurate information, purposefully and intentionally, and the importance of recognizing such disinformation (Bergstrom & West, 2020). The authors call out "obfuscation" (p.39) as a tactic to hide facts. They comment that bullshit is "intended to persuade or impress an audience by distracting, overwhelming, or intimidating them with a blatant disregard for truth, logical coherence, or what information is actually being conveyed" (p. 40). Another book, *Science Denial*, discusses how educators, science communicators, and others, can address deep-seeded denial (Sinatra & Hofer, 2021).

Beliefs that lead to denial are deeply held. They are often reinforced at home through years of indoctrination and the morass of disinformation that is spread through public and social media, depending on the reliability of sources (Bergstrom & West, 2020). Neil deGrasse Tyson, the astrophysicist, has commented that smart people are able to modify their thinking if newly acquired information provides contradictory evidence. In contrast, people who have been indoctrinated lack the ability to correct their thinking even when confronted with new information. They summarily dismiss facts and evidence, having been conditioned to do so. As McIntyre (2021) notes, in a book about counteracting denial, it is extremely difficult to change people's minds and beliefs. He cites the foundations from cognitive research that include cherry-picking, conspiracy theories, reliance on fake experts, logical errors, and unmet expectations for science.

Science is not the only content area in which denial occurs. History is another prominent domain. Deniers will refute that historical events ever happened, trying to recreate a dialogue around actual and real events.

And today society is ripe with conspiracy theories. The Holocaust is perhaps the most prominent event where even historians have denied it ever happened. One of the most blatant denials is recounted by Ambassador Deborah Lipstadt (2006), who was sued, as well as her publisher. Because the lawsuit occurred in Great Britian, the onus was on her to prove the Holocaust happened, which she did. The individual who sued her was a credentialed historian from England.

It may be even more difficult to instructionally and through classroom management practice find effective strategies to mitigate a denial situation. Discussions could get heated and even violent. Educators are likely to be aware of which topics may elicit problems. There are some possible strategies, but they may go only so far. Educators can help students evaluate the evidence and the sources from which the information comes. They should politely question if sources are reliable or biased. Have the students explain their rationales and thinking, but do not mock them, as difficult as that may be to show restraint. They can help students to recognize the deliberate attempt to manipulate and skew information. They can be made aware of confirmation bias, the trend to believe things based on your own perspective. Educators can help students to consider alternative hypothesis, triangulate across multiple sources of information, and consider if claims are too good to be true. Educators can help students to recognize expertise. This goes beyond data literacy to also include information and media literacy (Literat et al., 2021). In discussions or assignments, students should be made to provide a defense of their perspectives and the sources they have consulted. They should avoid sites known for manipulating facts and using superficial analysis. Students should be encouraged to identify alternative facts and fake news. As Sinatra and Hofer (2021) state: "Facts alone are not knowledge; and knowledge is not understanding. Knowledge requires justification and truth; individuals need to substantiate the information they have gleaned in order to truly know it" (p. 36).

References

Bergstrom, C. T. & West, J. D. (2020). *Calling bullshit: The art of skepticism in a data-driven world.* Random House.

Collins, F. S. (2024, September 22). Facts matter, and they don't care how you feel. *New York Times*. https://www.nytimes.com/2024/09/20/opinion/covid-vaccines-truth-life-death.html?smid=nytcore-ios-share&referringSource=articleShare&sgrp=c-cb&ngrp=mnp&pvid=A8EF4D4E-D518-474D-8ECD-26DD1955ECEC

Goldstein, D. (2024, September 22). How history teachers navigate the political divide. *New York Times*. https://www.nytimes.com/2024/09/19/us/social-studies-curriculum.html?smid=nytcore-ios-share&referringSource=articleShare&sgrp=c-cb&ngrp=mnp&pvid=92700A7E-6EC0-48A7-9E0B-C8E1D19AD3F9

Kavanaugh, J. & Rich, M. D. (2018). *Truth decay: An initial exploration of the diminishing role of facts and analysis in American public life*. RAND Corporation.

Literat, I., Chang, Y. K., Eisman, J., & Gardner, J. (2021). LAMBOOZLED!: The design and development of a game-based approach to news literacy education. *Journal of Media Literacy Education, 12*(1), 56–66.

Lipstadt, D. E. (2006). *History on trial: My day in court with a Holocaust denier*. Harper Perennial.

Mandinach, E. B. & Gummer. (2021a). Data ethics: An introduction. In E. B. Mandinach & E. S. Gummer (Eds.), *The ethical use of data in education: Promoting responsible policies and practices* (pp. 1–32). Teachers College Press.

McIntyre, L. (2021). *How to talk to a science denier: Conversations with flat earthers, climate deniers, and other who defy reason*. MIT Press.

Sinatra, G. M. & Hofer, B. A. (2021). *Science denial: Why it happens and what to do about it*. Oxford.

Villagran, L. (2024, September 15). How do we respond to election theories? *Arizona Republic*. https://arizonarepublic-az.newsmemory.com/?token=39d5e20a71a6066dd18bb3f661f33b74&cnum=7646d942-26d2-e711-b65f-90b11c343abd&fod=1111111-0&selDate=20240916&licenseType=paid_subscriber&

Bullying

Learning Objectives

- Learn about the potentially harmful consequences of students misusing social media.

- Consider the ramifications of bullying, whether in person or done electronically.
- Consider where responsibility lies if the bullying occurs outside of school or inside the school.

Scenario

Winchester is a community that has recently been experiencing various kinds of bullying events, both in-person and through social media. It is affecting all levels of the school district, but particularly the middle and high schools. The bullying has taken several different forms and courses of action varying in severity.

A first form is found among the schools' athletes where there are high expectations in terms of performance. Following games where certain athletes have not had good games, the social media accounts have exploded with not only negativity, but blatant threats. This is not unlike professional athletes who have experienced similar issues.

A second form emanates from a group of boys who have been cyberbullying girls in their schools. They are known as keyboard tough guys. In one incident, a girl ghosted the boys who had been harassing her. The boys then proceeded to do physical damage to the property of the student's family. The boys launched fireworks into a structure on the family property and burned it down, doing significant monetary damage. Luckily, no one was hurt, but property was destroyed. This was all in retaliation for the girl ghosting them. The school was aware of the harassment. (This incident actually occurred.)

A third form of bullying is in-person with taunting and some physicality, sometimes followed by electronic messages. The bullying can be a one-time event, but most often it is continuous.

Parents of the bullied students have taken their complaints and concerns to both school officials and the police, given that some of the incidents have occurred on school property and others off campus. A good deal of finger-pointing has occurred with no one taking responsibility for the situation. In fact, the police ignored a number of the reported incidents until the one that caused property damage, due to the level of severity.

Discussion Questions

- Do you think the responsibility lies with the school district?
- Do you think the responsibility lies with the parent or both parents?

Probing Questions

- Explain what culpability the school officials have in these incidents.
- Consider what differences it might make if an incident occurs on campus or off campus.
- Describe how you would handle a situation in which you discovered a bullying incident.
- Discuss the culpability of the parents in trying to control bullying incidents, especially repeated ones.
- Describe how you would work with the students who are being bullied and their parents.

Discussion of the Ethical Considerations

Bullying is on the rise. In the past, bullying was likely to be physical or verbal. Now there is an uptick in cyberbullying, where students attack other students using social media and email, sometimes anonymously or mostly known. It can lead to substantial harm and even suicide on the part of the targeted student. Bullying often is about the dominance of one individual or student over another. Bullies often lack empathy. They may be modeling behavior they have observed in their home environment. However, the focus of responsibility is still up for debate.

References

Brück, M. (2022, March 1). Athletes and social media: A double-edged sword. *DW*. https://www.dw.com/en/why-social-media-can-be-a-double-edged-sword-for-athletes/a-60874573

Cantone, E., Piras, A. P., Vellante, M., Preti, A., Daníelsdóttir, S., D'Aloja, E., & Bhugra, D. (2015). Interventions on bullying and cyberbullying in schools: A systematic review. *Clinical Practice and Epidemiology in Mental Health: CP & EMH, 11*(Suppl 1 M4), 58.

Cyberbullying Research Center. (n.d.). *Student athletes and social media*. Author. https://cyberbullying.org/student-athletes-social-media

Dominguez, M. (2025, February 23). Recorded confession could influence outcome of Gilbert barn fire case. *Arizona Republic*. https://www.azcentral.com/story/news/local/gilbert/2025/02/23/gilbert-barn-fire-case-teenager-accused-arson/76736550007/

Dominguez, M., & Avery, C. (2024, August 5). "Like sharks circling you": Parents detail of a year of intimidation leading up to Gilbert barn-burning. *Arizona Republic*. https://www.azcentral.com/story/news/local/gilbert/2024/08/05/teen-boys-burn-barn-create-havoc-in-gilberts-morrison-ranch/74430382007/

Teaching Art History

Learning Objectives

- Learn to consider how the same data points or lesson materials can be interpreted in different ways by different people with different perspectives.
- Gain an understanding that students will bring differing backgrounds and perspectives that will influence how they perceive instructional materials.

Scenario

Ms. Clarice teaches history at Summer High School. One of her units pertains to the history of the arts, including art history and music history. An objective for the unit is to help her students understand how historical events are interrelated with culture, religion, and the context of the times and emerge as themes in literature, art, architecture, and music. The course is really about world and historic culture.

Ms. Clarice prepares a slide deck that includes photos of classic art pieces and masterpieces. The deck is eclectic in that it spans a broad range of art media as well as topics, historical eras, and genres. Among them is

Michelangelo's statue of David. There is a picture of the prophet, Mohammed. There is also Picasso's Guernica, which is a deeply moving anti-war painting. Other potentially controversial pieces of art are included. Not all pieces are controversial, instead focusing on what society was like during certain historic eras.

Ms. Clarice leads the class through a discussion about the context during which the pieces of art were created. For example, Guernica focuses on a bombing incident during the Spanish Civil War. Goya's The Third of May shows the massacre of civilians in 1808. Less controversial works are shown, like Seurat's Sunday Afternoon on the Island of La Grande Jatte, which depicts Parisians in the 1880s enjoying an afternoon outing. Ms. Clarice provides her students links to some of the world's greatest art collections, like the Metropolitan Museum, the Louvre, the Prado, and the Hermitage. As a homework assignment, she asks the students to select one of the pieces of art shown or another that they may have found on the websites and asks them to write a brief essay about why they thought the piece was noteworthy in the context of the historical period and what were some of the societal, political, and historic foundations for the creation.

A few days after the class, Ms. Clarice was asked to come to the office and meet with the principal, Ms. Dulci. Apparently several parents complained to the building administration that the lesson was inappropriate, citing the content as too controversial, obscene, and upsetting.

Discussion Questions

- What do you think Ms. Clarice's response should be?
- How do you think Ms. Dulci should respond to the parents?

Probing Questions

- Discuss the intentions of the unit.
- Consider how history is being taught using this technique.
- Discuss whether the parents have any grounds for objecting to the classic pieces of art?
- Discuss how different students might perceive the various pieces of art differently from their own perspectives.

- Discuss the implications of deeming classic pieces of art, music, or literature inappropriate, obscene, or disturbing.
- Discuss whether it matters if the questionable pieces of art are considered masterpieces or not.

Discussion of the Ethical Considerations

In the past few years, using art in instructional venues has come under attack. At the college level, a professor was fired for showing a masterpiece, with forewarning to students, that offended the Muslim students in the class. Students complained, and the professor was fired, but later reinstated, and the university president forced to resign over how the situation was handled. In Florida, there was a controversy over the statue of David, and a principal was forced to resign. Memes of the statue with Florida covering the offending body parts were widely circulated because parents deemed this masterpiece to be obscene. A painting such as Guernica is known to be both highly controversial and emotionally laden due to the horrific scene it depicts. Part of the beauty of art is that different people will interpret it differently based on their own world views. The same data or stimulus elicit different reactions and different understandings and interpretations. Some art is intended to stimulate deep analysis and thought, others to generate emotions, or others simply for visual enjoyment.

There are a number of questions to be considered here. One involves censorship. Do parents have a right to demand the removal of certain content from instruction? What if it is the school board or the state department of education that objected to content? Who has the right to deem content objectionable? From a data perspective, this example shows the importance of considering divergent views from the same content. I like to use the Seurat example when I speak about different perspectives from the same data. Sunday Afternoon on the Island of La Grande Jatte is a pointillist painting, which means that instead of brushstrokes, the painting consists of strategically placed dots that form the figures. If you look at the painting closely, all you see are different colored dots. But as you step back and farther back, the painting comes into focus. That is similar to looking at data from differing points of view. Close up, the data may look one way; from afar, the data may look very different.

References

Patel, V. (January, 2023a). After lecturer sues, Hamline University walks back its "Islamophobic" comments. *New York Times.* https://www.nytimes.com/2023/01/17/us/hamline-lawsuit-prophet-muhammad-religion.html

Patel, V. (2023b January). A lecturer showed a painting of the Prophet Muhammad. She lost her job. *New York Times.* https://www.nytimes.com/2023/01/08/us/hamline-university-islam-prophet-muhammad.html

Solomon, T. (2023, April 6). Florida department of education declares 'artistic value' of Michelangelo's David amid controversy. *ARTnews.* https://www.artnews.com/art-news/news/florida-department-of-education-declares-artistic-value-of-michelangelos-david-amid-controversy-1234663232/

Sanewashing

Learning Objectives

- Learn how to discern fact from fiction.
- Understand how the use of "so-called" facts can be used in harmful ways.
- Understand that the validity or veracity of information is important in the educational process.
- Understand the importance of data literacy, information literacy, and media literacy.
- Recognize the potential consequences and harms.

Scenario

Mr. Rusty is a social studies teacher at Loki Middle School. He has been teaching for a long time and has seen the evolution of technology and online resources. He has been concerned about the lack of vetting of these sources, unlike the old-fashioned encyclopedias where you had confidence in the content. He recognizes that his students need a lesson about critical thinking skills that can help them to be able to consider what is true and what is false, and determining information from disinformation or misinformation. He develops a technique that he thinks will get this issue across to his students, drawing from the current political landscape and vocabulary. He intends to use "sanewashing" as a way to confront the students with topics that may be plausible, others that may be implausible, but all of which have outrageous descriptions that become sanitized. The objectives for the students are for them to be able to wade through the morass of junk and determine the veracity of the information despite reading commentaries that affirm and sanitize the misinformation.

Mr. Rusty discusses his strategy with some of his colleagues. Mr. Henry thinks it is a great teaching technique. Ms. Winnie is a bit more hesitant, given the divisive political environment where society is bombarded with misinformation and disinformation and that media are accused of sanitizing statements. Mr. Rusty notes her concerns and replies that this is precisely why the students need to understand the issue and apply critical thinking skills. He decides to try out the lesson. He develops documents that contain total inaccuracies. He finds news articles that contain falsehoods and have been sanewashed. He presents them to his students.

Discussion Questions

- What do you think of the instructional strategy?
- Do you agree with Ms. Winnie's concerns?

Probing Questions

- Discuss the pros and cons of the instructional technique.
- Discuss whether you think the students will be able to wade through the inaccuracies.
- Discuss the role of critical thinking in being able to verify credible and dubious sources of information.
- Explain how media literacy may influence students' ability to work through the exercise.
- Discuss what objections or limitations there may be to this exercise.
- Discuss whether you think the students will get it, understanding the instructional objectives.
- Consider both the intended and unintended consequences and the potential harms.

Discussion of the Ethical Considerations

Understanding fact from fiction has become an increasingly important part of data, information, and media literacy given that society is being bombarded by fake news and inaccuracies in various media. Data ethics play a big part; that is, knowing what data or information are real and appropriate in a given situation. While there is limited vetting for veracity of many online sources, it becomes increasingly important for students to use critical thinking to question things that do not make sense. As Judge Judy frequently says, "don't pee on my feet and tell me it's raining." Students and adults turn to their trusted sites and resources, which often serve to confirm their existing beliefs. This is confirmation bias. These sites may intentionally distort information or simply use no vetting processes. Even with the best intentions, inaccuracies can creep through. When asked about the vetting process at CNN, Anderson Cooper (2021) said that they put every story through three sets of accuracy checks, yet sometimes they still get it wrong. Judy Woodruff (2024) of PBS echoed a slightly different message by saying that the responsibility for vetting lies not only with the media but also with the consumers, hence the need for media literacy.

Professor Ionna Literat (Literat et al., 2021) at Teachers College has studied how children can learn to discern fact from fiction. She developed a game to teach media literacy that helps middle and high school students discern fake news through the use of game-based design. One can ask, if students can acquire appropriate skills, why not the general population?

Clearly, students can learn to use information responsibly. The flip side that pertains to ethics is when individuals intentionally skew data or information for inappropriate purposes. We see this in many disciplines—deceptive advertising, news, politics, law, and elsewhere (Mandinach & Gummer, 2021a). The key role education can play is to help children begin to understand the importance of using data and information properly and how to discern inappropriate use—fake news, skewed data, and disinformation.

References

Bertrand, M. & Marsh, J. A. (2015). Teachers' sensemaking of data and implications for equity. *American Educational Research Journal, 52*(5), 861–893.

Cooper, A. (2021, February 25). *Arizona speakers series* [Speech transcript]. https://arizonaseries.com.

Literat, I., Chang, Y. K., Eisman, J., & Gardner, J. (2021). LAMBOOZLED!: The design and development of a game-based approach to news literacy education. *Journal of Media Literacy Education, 12*(1), 56–66.

Mandinach, E. B. & Gummer, E. S. (2021a). Data ethics: An introduction. In E. B. Mandinach & E. S. Gummer (Eds.), *The ethical use of data in education: Promoting responsible policies and practices* (pp. 1–32). Teachers College Press.

Nickerson, R. S. (1998). Confirmation bias: A ubiquitous phenomenon in many guises. *Review of General Psychology, 2*(2), 175–220.

Woodruff, J. (2024, February 29). *Arizona speakers series* [Speech transcript]. https://arizonaseries.com

Science Isn't About Beliefs

Learning Objectives

- Learn that science uses real data and evidence, not beliefs and gut feelings.
- Understand the ramifications of introducing beliefs into scientific reasoning.

Scenario

Mr. Beau is a science teacher at Summer Middle School. He has prepared a lesson on experimental design. Part of the lesson is to have students pose hypotheses, examine the differences between control and experimental groups, draw conclusions, and make interpretations based on the results. A computer simulation program will present the data so that the students can make manipulations and see the outcomes. The topics of the simulations are based on content that the class has already covered in their textbooks and in open discussion. Thus, the students are already familiar with the material.

Mr. Beau asks students to state their hypotheses. One student, Fred, begins his hypothesis with, "I believe…." Another student, Ethel, says, I think. . . . Mr. Beau stops the discussion right there. He questions both students and has them explain their thinking. Fred fails to provide a defensible rationale whereas Ethel bases her comments on what she read in the textbook.

Mr. Beau then has the students run the simulation. This time he asks students to interpret the results and tie them to their hypotheses. Bob says, "The data support my hypothesis and here is why. Hazel counters by saying she disagrees and believes the results do not make sense.

Discussion Questions

- What do you think about the use of "think" versus "believe"?
- What do you think about Mr. Beau's instructional strategy?

Probing Questions

- Discuss what role beliefs play in science.
- Discuss the ethics of making scientific or other kinds of interpretations based on beliefs as opposed to data and evidence.
- Discuss the intentions of trying to elicit from students an understanding and appreciation of using data to inform interpretations.

Discussion of the Ethical Considerations

Science is about using data or evidence to make interpretations. Ethical data use is about using the "right" data and the "right" analytics to draw conclusions that are based on sound evidence from which interpretations and decisions can be made. Beliefs have no role here. Confirmation bias is about using one's beliefs to skew the use of evidence. Often decisions are made based on assumptions, beliefs, gut feelings, anecdotes, limited data, the wrong data, or using inappropriate analytics. This is an important lesson to convey to students and for teachers to use in their own practice. Use data, not opinions, beliefs, or assumptions.

References

Bertrand, M. & Marsh, J. A. (2015). Teachers' sensemaking of data and implications for equity. *American Educational Research Journal, 52*(5), 861–93.

Sinatra, G. M. & Hofer, B. A. (2021). *Science denial: Why it happens and what to do about it.* Oxford.

Classroom Monitoring

Learning Objectives

- Understand the privacy and ethical issues of having electronic monitoring in classrooms.
- Consider the implications of interpreting or misinterpreting the data that results from the technology.

Scenario

The Norman School District adopted the use of classroom monitoring and management software and e-proctoring technology during the pandemic to help educators see what was happening with their students through their devices. There were pros and cons to the technology. Teachers were able to see student work. But they were also able to observe student behavior, inappropriate activities, and things going on in the background, including home conditions (i.e., evidence of neglect, abuse, illegal activity). Through the e-proctoring software, teachers were able to detect possible cheating on tests.

Following the pandemic, the technologies were transferred to the classrooms. In the wake of both venues, Dr. Gentoo, Norman's superintendent, received a flurry of complaints from parents about how student behavior was misinterpreted as well as about violations of student and family privacy. One parent complained that a concern had been raised about bruises seen on a student. Another parent had been questioned over a concern about possible neglect because the student had appeared on camera, and later in the classroom, disheveled and in filthy clothing. One student had been caught talking to someone during an online assessment. All of these issues raised concerns for the parents.

Discussion Questions

- What do you think about using such technology to monitor student behavior?
- Does it make a difference whether the technology is being used in the home setting or in a classroom?

Probing Questions

- Discuss the privacy ramifications of using such software.
- Discuss the pros and cons of using such technology.
- Discuss some of the potential for misinterpreting the data.
- Discuss how Dr. Gentoo should respond to the parental complaints.

Discussion of the Ethical Considerations

The use of technologies, particularly those that are AI-generated, gained prominence during the pandemic. Schools had to rely on technology for the delivery of instruction and the collection of student performance. A byproduct of some of the technologies was the capacity to surveil a student's environment, not only observe student performance. The teacher could see facial expressions and body movements that might indicate a level of engagement or disengagement in the instructional activity. A teacher could also see what was going on in the background, for better or for worse. The teacher might observe some environmental threats such as someone doing drugs, a child with bruises, family discord, indications of neglect, and much more. This kind of monitoring raises ethical questions, with the potential for bias, intrusiveness, and privacy violations, especially if the interpretations are inaccurate. Even though the technology is well intended, there could be unintended consequences and potential harm. What if the teacher reported a possible threat to a student based on observations and it turned out to be nothing? This could be true in classroom instruction as well. One has to question if the observations have validity? Are the data accurate? How are they being used and for what purposes?

One such incident made the news in 2021 and was mentioned in Chapter 3. The Dartmouth Medical School used technology to give students assessments. The technology proctored the students while taking the examinations. The technology identified certain body movements and eye movements that may be an indication of cheating. Given that data, students were expelled from the institution. Ultimately the students were reinstated because the interpretations of the data were flawed. Imagine a student reaching for a tissue or a cup of coffee. The technology may have flagged the movement as a student reaching for some means of cheating. Similarly with eye movements, a student could look away from the screen to see something happening in their environment (i.e., the phone ringing, the doorbell dinging, an animal jumping on to the desk, or something else) and that could be flagged as a violation.

The data have to make sense. And educators need to use caution. Yet as a mandated reporter, teachers also must be vigilant about reporting potential harm to students if there is a reasonable amount of suspicion, whether in person or via electronic media. What should an educator do if he or she sees something that is a real threat to the student like a gun, violence, or a child who shows apparent signs of neglect? What is the balance between diligent observation in contrast to over-surveillance and violations of privacy?

References

Holmes, W. (2023, October). The unintended consequences of artificial intelligence and education. *Education International*. https://discovery.ucl.ac.uk/id/eprint/10179267/

Holmes, W. & Tuomi, I. (2022). The state of the art and practice in AI in education. *European Journal of Education*, 57(4), 542–70.

Singer, N. & Krolik, A. (2021, May 9). Online cheating charges upend Dartmouth Medical School. *New York Times*. https://www.nytimes.com/2021/05/09/technology/dartmouth-geisel-medical-cheating.html

Electronic Essay Scoring

Learning Objectives

- Understand how the underlying algorithms and databases may privilege some students at the expense of others.
- Consider how language norms may differ across cultural groups.

Scenario

The Sampson School District adopted AI technology to score student essays. The technology is based on an extensive database that scores the essays on content, style, grammar, and detail. The scoring does not address potential plagiarism. The language arts department begins using the program, and the teachers come together to discuss what they think about it. The department chair, Ms. Emma, has the teachers conduct analyses of the results and compare them to how they would have scored the student work.

One teacher, Ms. Stella, concurs with the electronic scores. Another teacher, Mr. Thor, agrees for the most part. But Ms. Freya notes a potentially disturbing trend that she sees among her students. Some students are being penalized for writing shorter essays than other students. If she were grading, she would have graded differently because the students have made their points through succinct or even terse writing. Ms. Freya wonders if the technology is somehow biased against the length of writing. She further notes that those who are writing shorter essays come from one particular group of language speakers. Another teacher, Mr. Smudge notes another possible issue. He mentions that the software has failed to pick up nuances of reasoning or variations in vocabulary usage.

Discussion Questions

- What do you think of the district's decision to adopt the technology?
- What do you think of the teachers' discussion?

Probing Questions

- Discuss what some of the ethical ramifications of using the electronic scoring versus scoring by the teachers.
- Discuss whether you think there might be differential impacts on some students based on their demographics or other characteristics.
- Discuss what you think the department should do regarding the continued use of continuing to use the technology.

Discussion of the Ethical Considerations

Technologies such as electronic essay scoring programs are only as good as their algorithms and the database from which they make decisions. Large testing organizations such as Educational Testing Service have been using and testing machine scoring for over a decade (Bridgeman et al., 2012). I had a conversation with one of the ETS authors, who told me about results in which Asian students wrote essays whose length, writing style, and specificity differed from those of other groups of students with consequences for their scores. She mentioned issues around length and standard English versus what might be considered non-standard English (personal communication, C. Trapani, May 3, 2024). She noted things about the underlying models. For example, AI models are probability-based whereas algorithms are decision-making-based. She questioned whether the use is for advocacy or for objective reporting, high-stakes or not, and whether there was test preparation or not. There are also cultural differences. Asian cultures have different perspectives about helping someone on a test, thus cheating has a cultural component.

There are many other concerns with machine scoring that could bias the results. One can question what is considered good writing and whether the technology can discern some of the identified characteristics. The National Council of Teachers of English (NCTE) (2013) notes elements such as logic, clarity, organization, use of evidence, humor, creativity, and other features. NCTE also mentions length and characteristics such as spelling, grammar, and punctuation, which are deemed structural.

These issues should raise questions about the accuracy of scoring as well as whether there could be potential harm to certain groups of students. These are not only technical questions about the data and results, but also ethical because of the possibility of differentially impacting some students over others.

References

Bridgeman, B., Trapani, C., & Yigal, A. (2012). Comparison of human and machine scoring of essays: Differences by gender, ethnicity, and country. *Applied Measurement in Education, 25*(1), 27–40.

NCTE. (2013, April 20). *NCTE position statement on machine scoring.* https://ncte.org/statement/machine_scoring/

Data Dashboards

Learning Objectives

- Understand the purposes of data dashboards and early warning systems.
- Understand the potential limitations to the data contained in the systems.

Scenario

The Winston School District has adopted early warning systems and data dashboards to provide educators with easily accessible data about students who have been identified as being at risk for failure and dropping out. Data are collected throughout the middle school years and into early high school. Four indices are presented to teachers on a data dashboard. These indices have been shown through research to predict which students are most likely to drop out or be at risk of dropping out. The indices are the number of absences, the number of failed classes, insufficient credits, and low GPA. The dashboard provides freshmen teachers with alerts about students who have one or more of the indicators. School administrators and counselors also provide educators with a list of targeted students.

Teachers convene to consider appropriate strategies and interventions that may be used to address student needs. They score the list of students who are categorized by the number of indicators, with four being the most challenging. Some teachers shrug at the students who have all four indicators and question what they can possibly do to help these kids. One teacher, Ms. Bhindi, mumbles an aside about whether it is even worth trying; these kids are too far gone. Perhaps their attention is better served elsewhere where they can make a difference. Other teachers focus on the students with only one indicator, trying to identify strategies that might be more easily addressed, like figuring out how to get students to school. They consider the actionability of the data. Mr. Oliver considers the issue of absenteeism and throws out various ideas about the reasons why students may not be attending school. But he questions what they, as teachers can do.

Discussion Questions

- What do you think about the use of early warning data?
- What do you think about the four indicators?
- What are your thoughts about the actionability of some data?

Probing Questions

- Discuss the ethics of focusing on these four indicators. What other data might be informative?
- Discuss the potential over-reliance on this data.
- Discuss the potential harms and benefits for students.
- Discuss how teacher discourse evolved. What do you think about the strategy of focusing on students with only one indicator and giving up on those with four?
- Discuss whether you consider these indicators sufficient from which to make consequential decisions about challenged students.
- Discuss whether students with four indicators are being labeled and sorted.

Discussion of the Ethical Considerations

Graduation rates and dropout rates have become key accountability metrics for schools and districts. Therefore, finding ways to increase graduation rates and mitigate those who may drop out are important to educators. It is therefore essential to understand the contributing factors to dropping out, not just looking at the numbers.

Research clearly has shown that indicators such as those mentioned above are related to students deemed at risk for dropping out of school. Snipes and Tran (2015) identified these four indices, but they also noted the importance of looking at the role of mindset in dropping out, a very different kind of data. The four indices are likely to be contained in district data warehouses, but mindset data, not so likely. Take, for example, the variable, the number of absences which is a hard data point, a number. We are aware that districts have a targeted number above which a student is labeled chronically absent. What that number does not explain is the reason for the absences. Are they medically related? Are they related to a student who simply cannot get out of bed due to laziness? Perhaps the student has had to work all night to support the family and is exhausted. The absences could be because the student has no way to get to school either by public transportation, school transportation, or parents or guardians. The absences might be due to a lack of parental support or awareness. The indicator can provide an alert. Data or information that provide explanations may lead to possible solutions, often times by gaining assistance from social services or other agencies. It is ill-advised and premature to make decisions or assumptions without full knowledge of circumstances, the student's context, background, and home situation. Those data might not be directly actionable for the educators, but they can lead to the enlistment of appropriate support services and interventions. Thus, the key lesson here is to look beyond what may be more apparent in the data to try and understand the underlying conditions before acting.

References

National Forum on Educational Statistics. (2018). *Forum guide to early warning systems* (NFES2019035). U.S. Department of Education,

National Center for Educational Statistics. https://nces.ed.gov/pubs2019/NFES2019035.pdf

Snipes, J. & Tran, L. (2015). *Early indicators and academic mindsets in the Clark County School District.* REL -West@WestEd.

Disclosed or Undisclosed Heath Issue

Learning Objectives

- Consider the issues around protecting student privacy for topics such as health.
- Consider how regulations like FERPA come into play.
- Consider the consequences of decisions.

Scenario

Ms. Katie is trying to conduct a class at the Gizmo Middle School. There is an undercurrent as the class begins. She does not quite understand what is happening, so she directly asks Maya, who is looking somewhat sheepish. Maya responds by saying that Lily is suffering from an asymptomatic form of a certain disease. Ms. Katie looks stunned. Lily remains quiet. Ms. Katie tries to determine what the proper course of action is in the classroom. She is trying to process many questions at the same time. First, is it right for one student to disclose another student's medical condition, especially in front of an entire class? Second, is the report is accurate as she has seen no indications of anything wrong with Lily? Third, is this just an attempt to explicitly bully a student? Fourth, is this a tactic to disrupt the class? Fifth, is what Maya said real or false, and what should be done in either case?

Whatever the situation, Maya has successfully derailed the class for the day. Ms. Katie knows there are student privacy issues at risk here and must be very cautious in how she handles the class. She considers what to do next and to whom she should make some inquiries.

Discussion Questions

- What do you think of what happened in the class?
- What do you think Ms. Katie should do?
- What is your interpretation of Maya's revelation and Lily's lack of reaction?
- To whom do you think Ms. Katie should consult?

Probing Questions

- Discuss the consequences of Maya revealing Lily's health situation in public in class, whether it is real and if it is false.
- Consider the potential harms and violations of student privacy.
- Discuss how Ms. Katie and the school should protect Lily's privacy.
- Consider whom Ms. Katie should consult: Lily, the school nurse, building leadership, or Lily's parents?

Discussion of the Ethical Considerations

The disclosure of student health information is a tricky thing, as both FERPA (and less so with HIPAA) come into play depending on the circumstances. Even discussions between educators and the school nurse can be tricky. Some student health data are part of a student's record and can be disclosed to educators if there is a legitimate need to know.

In this scenario, there are many twists and turns. First, it is unclear whether the student in question actually has a medical issue or whether it has been falsified. Second, it is a student, and not the affected student, who has disclosed the issue. The teacher is hearing it second- or third-hand. And it has been announced to the whole class with no response from Lily, who could easily verify or deny the accusation. She may be embarrassed or complicit in the classroom hoax. It is hard to tell but Ms. Katie should err on the side of caution out of protection for Lily.

A first action Ms. Katie might take is to ask Lily to have a private discussion to determine whether there is a real issue or not. Ms. Katie could also contact Lily's parents and discuss what had happened in class and ask if there is a health issue or not. The parents could choose not to answer. To be super cautious, Ms. Katie might consult her principal or school nurse to determine how to proceed here. There are at least two issues. The first issue would be to obtain guidance on how to handle the verification of the health issue and how to deal with Lily. The second issue, which follows, is how to proceed with the class. Should Ms. Katie say anything to the class that does not violate Lily's privacy or choose to ignore the entire episode. Students are likely to say something if it is ignored. The main objective here is to protect the privacy of the student while also trying to seek the truth. Engaging other students or other teachers is ill-advised.

References

Mandinach, E. B. & Cotto, J., (2021). *Student privacy primer.* Future for Privacy Forum and WestEd. https://studentprivacycompass.org/resource/student-privacy-primer/

Mandinach, E. B., Jimerson, J. B., Siegl, J., & Sallay, D. (2023). *Student privacy primer for school leaders.* Future for Privacy Forum and WestEd.

Pronouns

Learning Objectives

- Understand the importance of student privacy.
- Understand the different protections for students of majority age as opposed to minors.
- Consider when parents need to be informed about their child.

Scenario

Pal and Abby are seniors at Roamie High School. Pal just turned 18, and Abby is 17. One of the classes they take is a hybrid; that is there are components carried on using Zoom whereas other components are in class. Mr. Wilbert is the teacher. He launches Zoom and the students log in. One of the first things he notices is that Pal's pronouns have changed from male to female. Abby's now reads "they/them." Mr. Wilbert says nothing and does nothing. Some of the other students also notice.

When the class resumes in person, there are some side conversations among student groups. Word somehow trickles back to the students' parents who become concerned. They request a meeting with Mr. Wilbert and Dr. Boomer, the principal. It is unclear if the parents had prior knowledge about the gender identity issue. They may or may not be upset, but they are concerned about the potential impact on their children.

Discussion Questions

- What do you think about this situation?
- Would you consider it an "outing" given that the students publicly changed their pronouns?
- Are there different privacy issues for the two students?

Probing Questions

- Discuss how Dr. Boomer and Mr. Wilbert should proceed in the discussions with the two sets of parents.
- Discuss the potential consequences of word getting back to the parents if they are not aware of the changes in gender identity.
- Discuss what the implications might be if the school officials contacted the parents.
- Discuss the ethical issues involved in this scenario.

Discussion of the Ethical Considerations

Student privacy regulations do indeed differ for students who are of majority age as opposed to those aged 17 and below. Parents do not need to be consulted for adult students. In fact, there are protections around majority students' privacy. So in this scenario, school officials technically do not have to speak with Pal's parents.

Educators need to consider the potential harms here. The students obviously went public by posting their pronouns. The parents may or may not have been aware of this fact. If they were unaware, then this could be considered disclosure of student information. It is likely, however, that they were aware and requested the meeting to discuss the potential fallout from other students. But what if the students were closeted and did not publicly self-identify and parents were notified? What then?

Take, for example, an article that appeared in *Slate* (Caraballo, 2022). This article described a student whose identity was detected through a school-based software program. School officials then contacted the student's parents and literally "outed" the individual. Are the parents entitled to know? Does it matter the age of the student? The school's explanation in the article was that notifying the parents was done to protect the student from bullying. Consider the plausibility of that explanation.

References

Baker, K. J. M. (2023, January 22). When students change gender identify and parents don't know. *New York Times.* https://www.nytimes.com/2023/01/22/us/gender-identity-students-parents.html?smid=nytcore-ios-share&referringSource=articleShare

Caraballo, A. (2022, February). Remote learning accidentally introduced a new danger for LGBTQ students. *Slate.* https://slate.com/technology/2022/02/remote-learning-danger-lgbtq-students.html

Ettinghoff, E. (2014). Outed at school: Student privacy rights and preventing unwanted disclosures of sexual orientation. *Loyola of Los Angeles Law Review, 47*(2), 1–42.

Office of Civil Rights. (n.d.). *Resources for LGBTQI+ students.* https://www2.ed.gov/about/offices/list/ocr/lgbt.html

Underlying App Data

Learning Objectives

- Help educators to be alert to the underlying data being generated by adopted apps.
- Alert educators to the inappropriate access to electronic data in apps or other technologies that may inadvertently occur.

Scenario

The Quinn School District has adopted some large-scale data warehouses where a plethora of student data is collected and stored. Additionally, teachers are encouraged to find innovative technologies and apps to use to enhance and make more engaging their classroom practices. There is an approval process, but sometimes some things fall through the cracks and potential problems are undetected.

Some of the teachers have adopted apps that collect data about nutrition, activity, and health. The data from these apps are intended to help students try to try and self-monitor to lead a healthy lifestyle. Mr. Buster, the physical education teacher, examines the students' activity levels. Mr. Ricky is one of the elementary school teachers who tries to help his students understand proper nutrition. Both of the teachers note some issues with certain students and they begin to discuss their concerns. They reach out to building leaders and the school nurse who can also examine the data as they are uploaded to one of the district data warehouses.

Mr. Buster and Mr. Ricky initiate conversations with some of the students where there are identified warning signs. The data may mean that the students are not receiving balanced meals, enough food, or too much food. Some may be too sedentary. Some are losing weight and others gaining weight. Both teachers ask for consultations with the school nurse, counselors, and building leaders.

As the "intervention" team is meeting, the principal, Ms. Beatrice, receives an alert from the IT department. One of the technology vendors somehow obtained access to the student health data and notified local healthcare providers who are subsequently offering low-cost medical assistance to the targeted students.

Discussion Questions

- What should Ms. Beatrice do about the potential leak of the student data?
- What do you think about the use of these kinds of data and technologies?

Probing Questions

- Consider the use of the apps even if the data were not leaked.
- Consider the potential benefits to students and the potential harms.
- Discuss what kinds of things educators can do with this data to assist students in need.
- Discuss whether you think the collection of this data are informative or intrusive and if they can be used for legitimate instructional and behavioral purposes.
- Discuss the implications surrounding the underlying mechanisms for data collection in such apps. Are there any concerns?
- Discuss the issues surrounding vendor access to student data.

Discussion of the Ethical Considerations

The apps that teachers were using were intended for educational purposes. The teachers hoped that students could benefit from the opportunity to self-monitor their data, and then the teachers could engage the students in fruitful discussions about healthy lifestyles. The strategy was a creative way to enhance more traditional instruction and make the information meaningful for the students. This was about the triangulation of multiple data sources. Where the situation turns is that unfortunate use of the data being collected by the apps, which the teachers could not have predicted. The vendors were wrong, even though they were trying to use the data to offer health services. It was an inappropriate use of the data.

Data breaches can happen on apps on mobile devices, but they also occur on district and state data warehouses. As an example, the Arizona state longitudinal data system was breached and student data accessed by a healthcare provider who sought to provide dental services to low-income students (Herold, 2014). These data were improperly accessed and used. This article recounts other breaches as the county, city, and district levels. The inadvertent release of personally identifiable information is both dangerous and a violation of FERPA.

References

Herold, B. (2014, January 22). Danger posed by student-data breaches prompts action. *Education Week*. https://www.edweek.org/policy-politics/danger-posed-by-student-data-breaches-prompts-action/2014/01

Mandinach, E. B., Cotto, J., Rastrick, E., Siegl, J., Vance, A., & Wayman, J. C. (2021, October). *Student data privacy and data ethics scenarios*. Future for Privacy Forum and WestEd. https://studentprivacycompass.org/resource/scenarios-user-guide/

Singer, N. (2013, October 5). Deciding who sees students' data. *New York Times*. https://www.nytimes.com/2013/10/06/business/deciding-who-sees-students-data.html?smid=nytcore-ios-share&referringSource=articleShare&sgrp=c-cb

Accountability

Learning Objectives

- Understand how to balance accountability pressure with continuous improvement that may benefit students.
- Consider the importance of including metrics beyond those used for accountability to help educators better understand and serve their students.

Scenario

The Bradley School District has done something quite risky. It has adopted the use of what are called graduate profiles. Some districts prefer the terms portrait or learner characteristics. The district has reached out to various stakeholder groups, especially employers, to understand what skills and knowledge they want future hires to exhibit. Many of the skills surprised administrators. It was not so much about content knowledge that would be observed through standardized test scores. Instead, the stakeholders thought skills and knowledge such as critical thinking, collaboration, communication, civic engagement, character, and wellness are essential for post-graduation performance. District administrators discuss how to integrate these skills into the curriculum. The discussion is telling. A deputy superintendent, Dr. Max, comments that not all students will apply to college, so attending to their needs is really important for student success. Dr. Grady counters with some concerns as the director of assessment. First, how will educators reliably and validly assess these new skills? Second, what impact will a shift in focus have on traditional accountability metrics on which the district is measured? The director of instruction, Dr. Poppy, notes that such a drastic change will require a mindset shift among the educators and some may push back and even leave. The district must provide lots of professional development and support, plus run interference if test scores are affected at least in the short term.

Mr. Joseph, the communications director, questions how the district should position the changes to the public because most people recognize test scores as the indicator of district success. Two of the high school principals, Ms. Elsie and Mr. Jeremy ask what they should do when parents pressure their faculty about college entrance requirements, test scores, and other metrics, like the International Baccalaureate. The concern is that their teachers will feel pressured and it might lead to some questionable practices, like gaming the system, teaching to the test, using past tests, and even manipulating results if the changes may cause test performance to decrease significantly.

Dr. Max reminds all of the convened leaders that accountability measures are only a small slice of education and what the district must attend to is what really matters: student success more broadly defined. He cautions that as long as test scores and the other traditional metrics do not decline and that the district shows other kinds of progress, then they all need to keep their eyes on the long-term objectives.

Discussion Questions

- What do you think about the issues raised in the scenario?
- What would you do as an educator in this situation?
- What if the best interest of the students or some students is in conflict with the traditional metrics of success? How do you balance that?
- What do you think about Dr. Max's perspective?

Probing Questions

- Discuss some of the ethical considerations raised here.
- Discuss the implications of using diverse data sources like those mentioned and the impact on the educational process and on the students.
- Discuss potential stresses for teachers that might force them into questionable actions.
- Discuss your thoughts about graduate profiles and learner characteristics.
- Discuss how you would handle conversations with parents or other stakeholders about the possible risks and challenges to the balance between accountability and continuous improvement.

Discussion of the Ethical Considerations

Accountability will always be part of the education process, and districts will always be measured by traditional metrics of success. It takes creative and innovative administrators to buck the system and to take calculated risks that may positively impact the students for long-term success. This means looking at broader indices of student success that will not only prepare them for higher education but success in life and in employment. Consulting and gaining the buy-in from stakeholder groups is a good strategy. What may be problematic is if teachers continue to feel pressured and try to game the system in some way because accountability is looming in the background. There is a need for support from administrators and the development of innovative strategies to address the concerns. It requires a mindset change among educators and broad systemic changes. A key here will be for the district to be completely transparent about the change process, the possible impacts, and the data that will be used and how progress will be monitored for the trajectory of improvement.

References

Gutman, L. M. & Schoon, I. (2013). *The impact of non-cognitive skills on outcomes for young people: Literature review*. Institute of Education, University of London.

Nichols, S. L. (2021). Educational policy contexts and the (un)ethical use of data. In E. B. Mandinach & E. S. Gummer (Eds.), *The ethical use of data in education: Promoting responsible policies and practices* (pp. 81–97). Teachers College Press.

Student Newspaper

Learning Objectives

- Understand that the appropriate use of data by students and educators is an important skill.
- Understand the ramifications of using "alternative facts" or eschewing credible evidence.

Scenario

Mr. Nugget is the advisor to the student newspaper at Kutsy High School. He has spent a good deal of time talking to the staff members about the responsibility of fact-checking and using appropriate journalism techniques. The paper is edited by two seniors, Eva and Bailey.

The paper has an edition soon to be published, and the staff is looking for an engaging topic. Millie and Dallas want to write a piece on an event that was somewhat controversial and involved both students and a few teachers. The editors assign the two reporters to do some research and conduct interviews as needed. Millie and Dallas request interviews with several students and teachers. The students, Coco, Layla, and Ollie willingly agree. The teachers, Mr. Taffer, Mr. Randolph, and Ms. Oliva are a bit more reluctant. Millie and Dallas develop a set of questions and conduct the interviews. They jointly write the article. What they did not do is share the draft article for review with those who were interviewed so that content and quotes could be verified.

When the paper is distributed, there is a lot of reaction throughout the school. In particular, Mr. Taffer and Ms. Oliva are visibly distressed, but Mr. Randolph is less so. The reporters have distorted what they said in their interviews in an apparent attempt to skew the data toward their own perspective. The teachers approach Mr. Nugget and ask for a meeting with the reporters, despite that the damage already having been done.

Discussion Questions

- What should Mr. Nugget do about the situation?
- What do you think about how the reporters used the data?
- What responsibility do you think the editors have for what the reporters wrote?
- Should the reporters have had the interviewees review the article before publication?
- What responsibility does Mr. Nugget have as a faculty advisor?

Probing Questions

- Discuss how Mr. Nugget should use the situation as a learning opportunity for the reporters and the editors.
- Discuss the recourse Mr. Taffer and Ms. Olivia have by asking for a retraction, given the rights of the reporters.
- Discuss what would have happened if the reporters had only interviewed the teachers, or only the students.
- Discuss the importance of fact-checking one's data.
- Discuss the potential harms of publishing fake news.
- Discuss the ethical issues presented here and what the newspaper staff should have done.
- Discuss the difference between misinformation and disinformation. What differences would there be if the reporter purposefully misrepresented the facts versus if it was unintentional?

Discussion of the Ethical Considerations

Fake news and alternative facts are just that. The use of them is inappropriate at best and violates the principles of responsible journalism. Mr. Nugget should make this a learning opportunity for all involved. A retraction could help to correct the inaccuracies, although the damage has already occurred. An apology to the teachers would also be recommended.

The reporters had a responsibility to fact-check the data and accurately reflect that information in their article even if it conflicted with their perspective. This is a case of not only purposefully cherry picking, but an actual misrepresentation of facts. The reporters had a responsibility to present the facts. The editors had a responsibility to oversee the veracity of the reporting. And the advisor had a responsibility to make sure it was accurate.

At the heart of this issue is the contrast between misinformation and disinformation. If the reporters simply misunderstood what the teachers had said, then that would be misinformation. It would have been an accidental event. In contrast, if the reporters purposefully misrepresented the interview information, that would be disinformation; that is, knowingly skewing the facts, perpetuating lies, and presenting fake news. Mistakes do happen in journalism. Anderson Cooper of CNN and Judy Woodruff of PBS, among others promote the need for fact checking and though vetting processes in reporting. And despite rigorous vetting, journalists still sometimes get it wrong. That is entirely different from journalists who show no regard for the facts and present stories that have no basis in evidence.

References

Cooper, A. (2021, February 25). *Arizona speakers series* [Speech transcript]. https://arizonaseries.com

Woodruff, J. (2024, February 29). *Arizona speakers series* [Speech transcript]. https://arizonaseries.com

Support Services

Learning Objectives

- Understand the importance of protecting student data privacy.
- Understand how the triangulation of data sources can be used for a positive impact.

Scenario

The Cooper School District serves diverse groups of students where parental income spans the full range. Many students, however, come from challenged homes where there are limited resources and support. This means that students must rely on Free and Reduced Lunch and weekend backpacks for food and proper nutrition. Some students also must rely on district transportation because their parents or guardians work multiple jobs and are unavailable to drive them to school.

Superintendent Houdi convenes a meeting of some district leaders to discuss how best to provide the much-needed services to these students. Superintendent Houdi asks the data director, Mr. Polo to generate lists of students who qualify for the Free and Reduced Lunch and backpack programs. He then requests a list of students who must take district transportation. The convened group reviews the lists and looks for overlaps. Dr. Houdi also asks for data on absences and health, thinking that those data might be informative.

The vice principal of Rollo Elementary School, Ms. Elsie, notes that a disproportionate number of absences can be found among the students who receive these services. But rarely are students absent on Friday, perhaps an indication that receiving the weekend backpacks are essential to student well-being. The nurse at Rollo, Ms. Lu, also comments that many of these students seek help and comfort from her on a regular basis.

Dr. Houdi takes in all of the comments. The group begins to discuss strategies for improving support for these students.

Discussion Questions

- What do you think of the discussion?
- Do you think all of the staff in the group have a right to the data being discussed, given the sensitive nature of the topics?
- Are there any data privacy issues to consider here?

Probing Questions

- Discuss how the administrators brought together different data sources to better understand the situation.
- Consider what other data sources might be included.
- Consider the ramifications of distributing the list of students receiving the support services.
- Discuss the linking of Free and Reduced Lunch data with the transportation data.

Discussion of the Ethical Considerations

Both transportation and Free and Reduced Lunch data should be protected from unauthorized users. Transportation data contain student addresses. Free and Reduced Lunch is seen as a proxy for socio-economic status and poverty. Therefore, administrators should be aware that sharing that data must be controlled. This is a student data privacy issue.

The idea of triangulating among data sources to try and understand the data is a good strategy. Bringing together diverse data sources often will enable educators to gain new insights into what is happening with students. Take, for example, the fact that students are less likely to be absent on Fridays. It is a reasonable hypothesis that students understand that if they are in school on Fridays, they can obtain their weekend backpack of food. If they are absent on Fridays, then the potential consequences are not eating and hunger. Thus, the examination of different data can lead educators to make decisions that are beneficial to the students, a good example of ethical data use.

References

Cooper, C. A. (2016, May). How school backpack programs help alleviate hunger in America. *U.S. News & World Report*. https://health.usnews.com/health-news/blogs/eat-run/articles/2016-05-24/how-school-backpack-programs-help-alleviate-hunger-in-america

Kurtz, M., Conway, K. S., & Mohr, R. D. (2020). Weekend feeding ("BackPack") programs and student outcomes. *Economics of Education Review*, *79*, 102040. https://doi.org/10.1016/j.econedurev.2020.102040

Surveys

Learning Objectives

- Understanding the use of proxies can be informative and valid.
- Consider the validity of data in terms of turnaround time for feedback.

Scenario

The Malcolm School District conducts surveys of student well-being. The objective of the surveys is to determine how students are feeling and to attempt to predict students who may be struggling in some way. District leaders such as Superintendent Quincy recognize that the constructs being measured in the surveys are seen as foundational to effective learning; that is, for students to achieve, they must be "in the right place" in terms of socio-emotional well-being. The surveys contain topics such as health, mental health, belonging, school safety, relationships with other students and with teachers, economic status, wellness, and socio-emotional well-being. The surveys are meant to provide information that can alert educators so that they can then develop actionable interventions if needed.

Dr. Josephine, the director of assessment, and Dr. Morty, the lead district psychologist, administer age-appropriate versions of the surveys across the grade levels. Data are collected by the vendor, analyzed, and summary reports are returned to the district. Reports come in different formats. There are individual level reports that help educator to identify particular students are defined as struggling. There are reports at different levels of aggregation; grade level, school level, and the entire district. Because of the complexity of the analytics, the survey results are not returned to the district for three to four months.

Discussion Questions

- Do you think the feedback cycle provides valid data of student well-being?
- What do you think of the idea of students responding via self-report about such sensitive topics as well-being?

Probing Questions

- Consider what other measures or proxies for well-being might provide more timely feedback.
- Discuss what you think about the use of snapshot data, especially for a construct such as well-being.

- Discuss how you might obtain data that capture the ongoing or continuous trends, rather than static data.
- Given that students are linked by ID so that administrators will know who they are if the need arises, discuss whether you think students will admit or confess to having issues with any of the topics.
- Discuss whether you think students might be more forthcoming in their responses if their results could not be linked back to them.

Discussion of the Ethical Considerations

Snapshot data only capture the status of a targeted construct at a specific point in time. Such data can provide valuable information for some kinds of decisions, but not for diagnosis and remediation. Further, given the sensitive nature of well-being data, it might be helpful to know not only the point in time, but also trends. Students change daily, even moment to moment.

An additional problem here is the delay in the return of the results. If students are struggling, at-risk, or even potentially suicidal, waiting several months to obtain the feedback is too late. There is a parallel in high-stakes standardized test scores. If teachers do not receive the results until the following school year, those data no longer reflect where the students are academically, as things will likely have changed over the summer. So the data are limited in their information value for instructional modifications. The data may be helpful for other kinds of decisions, however. Such data are often called post-mortem or dead on arrival.

Vendors are marketing well-being surveys, and their websites contain information about the validity and reliability of the instruments. As districts make decisions about the adoption of such measures, it is incumbent upon administrators to perform due diligence and vet then for appropriateness for their objectives and decisions as well as turn around time given the time sensitive nature of the data. Administrators may also want to consider what other measurement techniques and even proxies might be used in conjunction with the surveys or as stand-alone indices.

References

Furlong, M. J., Dowdy, E., Nylund-Gibson, K., Wagle, R., Carter, D., & Hinton, T. (2021, February). Enhancement and standardization of a universal social-emotional health measure for students' psychological strengths. *Journal of Well-Being Assessment, 4,* 245–67.

van Staaten, L. (2022, October). To improve students' mental health, schools take a team approach. *New York Times.* https://www.nytimes.com/2022/10/06/education/learning/student-mental-health-crew.html

Online Threat

Learning Objectives

- Consider the potential risks and harm if a possible risk is uncovered through social media.
- Consider when safety concerns should override personal privacy.

Scenario

McGregor Elementary School has always been a safe environment for students. The principal, Mr. Theo, has great relationships with the students and staff. His office is also open to parents who, for the most part, are supportive of how he runs the school.

Mr. Atticus is one of the physical education teachers. He is conducting a class for the sixth-grade boys. When he enters the gym, he observes a group of students huddled around their phones. Andrew, Kenny, Cole, Gary, and Simon are all staring at their devices and shaking their heads. Mr. Atticus walks over and asks if there is a problem. The boys are hesitant and quiet. Mr. Atticus persists. Finally, Cole shows Mr. Atticus his phone with an open social media post made by another sixth grade student, Luke. Mr. Atticus carefully reads the post and instructs the boys to shut down their phones. He asks them to begin some exercises while he moves to the side of the gym and contacts Mr. Theo. Mr. Atticus describes the post as a veiled and potential threat to the school and to himself.

Discussion Questions

- What do you think about the students sharing the post with the teacher?

- What do you think Mr. Atticus should have done.
- What do you think Mr. Theo should do?

Probing Questions

- Discuss whether the teacher should have had access to the student's phone and the issues around sharing information in the post.
- Discuss the potential harms here and the ethics around educators viewing students' social media.
- Discuss whether there are differences in perceiving a post where there is a possible threat versus one where there is not perceived problem.

Discussion of the Ethical Considerations

Typically, students should not be sharing other students' posts, emails, or texts. But this case is different. The students perceive that the post might be a problem. Sharing it with the teacher is the right thing to do. Educators are mandated reporters and if there is a credible threat or potential harm to a student, the teachers must act. Contacting the principal was a reasonable next step. Mr. Atticus could also have sought out the student but it was best to leave that to the school authorities which has access to the kinds of interventions that might be needed for the school for the student in question. If the post turns out to be nothing, then there has been no harm.

References

Barnes, K. (2015). The challenge of data privacy. *Educational Leadership*, 73(3), 40–4.

Johnson, A. F. (2018). When can you search a student's phone? *THE Journal: Transforming Education Through Technology.* https://thejournal.com/articles/2018/03/12/when-can-you- search.aspx

6

Second Set of Scenarios

Chapter Outline

Law Enforcement	118
Too Similar	121
Facts and Data Matter	123
Allergies	127
Belief in Students	129
Expectations	131
Masking	134
Inconsistently Late	138
Pressure	140
Considering Consequences	142
Metrics Matter	145
They Know It	149
Attributions and Confirmation Bias	151
Productive Time	153
Feedback	155
Embedded Messages	157
Challenge Assumptions and Interpretations	159
More Is Less	160
Fitbits and Apple Watches	163
Blind Spots	165
Second Chance	167

This second scenario chapter contains the remaining scenarios, including the following:

Law Enforcement
Too Similar
Facts and Data Matter
Allergies
Expectations
Belief In Students
Masking
Inconsistently Late
Pressure
Considering Consequences
Metrics Matter
They Know It
Metrics Made Public
Attributions and Confirmation Bias
Productive Time
Feedback
Embedded Messages
Challenge Assumptions and Interpretations
More Is Less
Fitbits and Apple Watches
Blind Spots
Second Chance

Law Enforcement

Learning Objectives

- Gain an understanding about the sharing of information with local law enforcement.
- Understand the issues around schools sharing data with law enforcement in terms of privacy regulations.

Scenario

The Turbo School District likes to think that it has a good relationship with local law enforcement as their protection and support have been important in maintaining school safety. The police department has been helpful in working with the district resource officers, so there is very much a symbiotic relationship. In fact, staff from both agencies socialize periodically, going for coffee or a beer.

The community has recently had an escalation of teenage issues that include the destruction of property, teen violence, bullying, larceny, and more. Several officers are discussing this at one of the social gatherings. Officers Barnaby and River commented about how the kids are becoming more and more brazen in some of the things they have been doing. The resource officers, CC and Chester comment that they too have been having issues on campus. They discuss the similarities of the events but stop short of discussing any individual students by name, with one exception. Barnaby mentions a recent incident where a student, Sanders, caused damage to some property during a school day. Sanders should have been in school but was clearly truant. However, Barnaby cannot prove this specific student was absent that day without the assistance of school attendance records. CC and Chester look at one another, hesitating on how to respond, unsure if and how they should handle this subtle request for student information. One of them says, let us get back to you. When the officers leave, CC says to Chester, I am not sure we can give them this information. Chester is hesitant as well and suggests they consult the school principal, Ms. Elena.

Discussion Questions

- What do you think CC and Chester should do?
- How should Ms. Elena respond?

Probing Questions

- Discuss the considerations about student privacy if the resource officers share the requested data with the police officers, or if they choose not to share it.

- Discuss the ethics of sharing protected data across agencies.
- Discuss whether the school should release the information to the police.

Discussion of the Ethical Considerations

There have been a number of incidents where there are questions about the appropriateness and legality of the interactions between justice and school officials in terms of sharing information, especially if it is personally identifiable information that is protected by FERPA. The incident that has received the most attention occurred in Pasco County, FL. The intention was to predict which students might become criminals based on specific student data indicators. The sharing of data was of such concern that the US Department of Education opened an investigation into the legality of the data sharing (McGrory & Weber, 2021). In a move to protect the privacy of student data, the school resources officers ultimately were denied access to the district's early warning system (Ellenbogen, 2021). Reddy (2020), writing for the Future for Privacy Forum's *Student Privacy Compass* site, (https://studentprivacycompass.org/pasco/) called the situation "predictive policing". The access of the data was leading to targeting students based on student record data although the intent was to identify students at risk from victimization. Reddy noted that there was no transparency and no accountability to students and parents. The practices were in violation of FERPA. Reddy also recommends that all school districts look carefully at their policies about the sharing of information with law enforcement and how their resource officers interface with other agencies. For further information, I encourage those interested to read the Reddy posting as it provides in-depth information about the topic in terms of data privacy and its implications for practice.

References

Bedi, N., & McGrory, K. (2020, November 19). Pasco's sheriff uses grades and abuse histories to label schoolchildren potential criminals: The kids and their parents don't know. *Tampa Bay Times.* https://projects.tampabay.com/projects/2020/investigations/police-pasco-sheriff-targeted/school-data/

Layton, D., & Shaler, G. (2019). *School-based policing in Maine: A study on school resource officers in Maine's public schools*. Maine Statistical Analysis Center. https://digitalcommons.usm.maine.edu/cgi/viewcontent.cgi?article=1002&context=maine_statistical_analysis_center

Reddy, A. (2020, December 18). The trouble with Pasco County's predictive policing polies. *Student Privacy Compass*. https://studentprivacycompass.org/pasco/

Too Similar

Learning Objectives

- Learn about the importance of triangulating data sources.
- Understand the importance of obtaining complete data.
- Understand that jumping to conclusions is not a good idea.

Scenario

Luna and Paisley are identical twins who attend Watson High School. They are both on the gymnastics team and are applying to colleges. They are also applying for scholarships. Both processes require that the applicants write various essays. The twins are receiving guidance from their coach, Ms. Annie, and their academic counselor, Mr. Tiger. Luna and Paisley begin drafting their essays and preparing other materials required for the college admission process. The twins worked independently on the materials. Although they may seek admission to the same institutions, their interests and potential majors differ. One of the essays they had to write was about an important life event that has been impactful. Another essay was about aspirations.

Watson provides a service to high school seniors. The school convenes a panel of teachers to advise the students on their essays, giving them feedback on how to strengthen them before the final submission process. The motivation for the panel is to level the playing field because some students can hire private coaches or they have super engaged parents who will provide feedback on the essays. The panelists provide informal yet constructive feedback.

The review process is initially blind to avoid any potential bias or conflict of interest. Names are then attached to the essay so the students will receive the feedback. The panelists are reviewing a number of essays from a few dozen students. The panelists examine the essays for content, appeal, structure, and level of engagement. As the panelists are reading, they note some uncanny similarities among two sets of essays and flag them. They wonder how the essays could be so similar, whether this is a case of plagiarism or collaboration.

Discussion Questions

- Given that the work products are college application essays, is this different from a class assignment?
- What should the panelists do?
- If your were a panelist, would you think this is a case of plagiarism? Collaboration? Or something else?

Probing Questions

- Discuss the possibility that the essays could be legitimately similar, given the life experiences of the twins.
- Discuss the possibility that the twins collaborated and how the panelists should handle the situation.
- Discuss the potential harms if the two sets of essays came from unrelated students as opposed to the twins.
- Discuss whether this is a case of plagiarism and what evidence with affirm or not.

Discussion of the Ethical Considerations

Collaboration on essays can be a cultural phenomenon. In some cultures, collaboration among students is accepted, whereas in other cultures, essays of this sort are expected to be the sole product of an individual. There are also other possible sources of input. Families that can afford college application guidance may have advisors that assist students in the preparation of their essays and other materials. They may suggest or reject topics and provide feedback on how to structure the essays. Parents have been known to structure and edit application essays.

Another explanation for the similarities comes from the fact that the identical twins are likely to have shared life experiences that are then reflected in the essays. It does not mean they copied one another, but rather than those life experiences emerged in both sets of essays. It is not only a plausible explanation, but also a reasonable one. Because of this situation, one strategy is for the panelists to discuss the essays with both students, perhaps helping the twins to find slightly different angles to the same experiences. There is a small likelihood that if the essays were too similar, the colleges to which they are applying could flag both essays, not realizing that they come from identical twins. The panelists could urge the twins to add different foci or a few other experiences to differentiate themselves. The worst case scenario would be for an institution that fails to do its due diligence and through using multiple sources of data may draw the wrong interpretations about the applicants. However, an overarching question might be whether this is really a case of plagiarism, a case of collaboration, or something else.

References

Alzahrani, S. M., Salim, N., & Abraham, A. (2011). Understanding plagiarism linguistic patterns, textual features, and detection methods. *IEEE Transactions on Systems, Man, and Cybernetics, Part C (Applications and Reviews), 42*(2), 133–149.

Naik, R. R., Landge, M. B., & Mahender, C. N. (2015). A review on plagiarism detection tools. *International Journal of Computer Applications, 125*(11), 16–22.

Facts and Data Matter

Learning Objectives

- Understand the importance of using facts rather than anecdotes, gut feelings, and assumptions.

- Appreciate that there can be multiple interpretations to the same data.
- Understand that there is a need to use complete data to provide a comprehensive picture of the situation.
- Recognize that using the wrong data can be harmful.

Scenarios

Ms. Twyla teaches earth sciences to freshman at Mocha High School. The school is located in the southwestern part of the country. One of the topics she is addressing with her classes is around climate change. This is an especially salient topic, given the location of the school. Each night, Ms. Twyla listens to the local weather and each night, one of the meteorologists, Skylar, presents the latest data on record temperatures. In a recent broadcast, Skylar notes that there were 113 consecutive days of over 100 degrees, but the most days in a year were in 2020 when there were nearly 150 days. Students have done some of their own research. In class, Sebastian adds another statistic – that there have been 70 days over 110 degrees while only a few years ago, that number was 30, so the number has literally doubled. Chloe adds that the low temperatures for each day are also setting record highs and that it is staying hotter longer with the latest 110 degree day on record by a long shot. Ms. Twyla wants her students to examine the trends and have a class discussion about climate change. Students are assigned to do some additional research from the local records.

Bubba notes that in 2023 in July alone, there were 31 consecutive days where the temperature rose above 110 and never fell below 90. Pearl notes that one year, the area went nearly two-thirds of a calendar year without rain. There was not one single monsoon that delivered precipitation. Other students, Lexie, Woody, and Jemma all present data from graphs found on local news stations' website. Sophie and Peaches who were collaborating commented that they thought last year felt worse than the current year. Wayne processed that comment and rather aggressively countered with, where are your data? You said you think. BW then pipes up and asks, how can there be climate change when the hottest day on record was two decades ago. BW failed to omit that the record was nearly eclipsed several times in the past two years. BW's comment stirred up some other students. Ava commented, there is no such thing as climate change. Maeve adds, that her parents say that climate change is a hoax, made up by politicians for their own purposes. Cookie insists that she has looked at some websites and done reading that also says that there is no climate change; it is made up. Frazier waves his hands and actually says, this is all bunk and storms out of the room.

The class is nearing the end of the period so Ms. Twyla tells the students to take a breath and asks them to do some more research and they would resume their discussion the next day. She also urges the students to be respectful of one another but to make sure that they are using research evidence from credible sources.

Ms. Twyla is grateful the class is over and retreats to the faculty lounge where she recounts to some colleagues about what happened in class. Ms. Willow and Mr. Isadore said they have experienced similar discussions in their science classes. Mr. Biscuit said he has had things like this happen in his social studies class, so it is not just science but a broader issue. The principal, Mr. Maximillian, happens to walk in and overhears some of the discussion. Perhaps a faculty meeting could be devoted to strategies to handle topics that might be contentious even though there are sound evidentiary bases for the sciences and social sciences.

Discussion Questions

- What do you think of the situation?
- How should Ms. Twyla and the other educators handle the classes, especially for students who reject the scientific evidence?
- What are some strategies the educators could use?

Probing Questions

- Discuss some of the issues that underlie resistance or the rejection of scientific evidence.
- Discuss what educators can do in their classes when confronted by students who blatantly reject the scientific or historical evidence.
- Discuss the need to use complete data when carrying out an investigation.

- Discuss the need to use the "right" data, not those that would be considered "alternative facts".
- Discuss how you think Mr. Maximillian can guide his teachers in the use of effective strategies to mitigate the rejection of evidence.
- Discuss what the school's position should be if some of the parents were to confront the teachers or the principal.
- Discuss how the teachers could illuminate issues around sources of information.

Discussion of the Ethical Considerations

Francis Collins (2024), the former director of the National Institutes of Health, wrote an opinion piece for the *New York Times*, trying to communicate the importance of using facts, not feelings or assumptions. In the article, Dr. Collins noted the growing and problematic trend around the distrust of scientific evidence. He further commented about the rise of alternative facts and the complete rejection of science around topics that may be politically motivated issues, such as Covid relief and climate change. Put very simply, Dr. Collins commented, "There is such a thing as truth, and truth matters" (p. 5).

There are a number of ways to engage in discussions without being accusatory or offensive. But that said, it is also very difficult to change peoples' minds when they are grounded in alternative and baseless theories. Teachers should not mock, attack, offend, or directly confront a denying student. The teacher might ask the student to provide evidence of the theory, noting what are the sources that that informed the thinking. The teacher could note that particular sites may not be credible but that only plays into the alternative perspectives.

Because of the pervasiveness of science denial and the general rejection of scientific evidence, a suggestion might be for the school to develop strategies to help science and social studies teachers deal with situations when students push back on the facts. These two departments are likely to be disproportionately impacted by denial. The school should also develop a strategy of how to handle parents who will likely confront the educators about topics like vaccination, climate change, evolution, and more. It is important for educators to remember that facts matter. Changing the thinking of deniers will be nearly impossible. So having strategies for respectful interactions may be helpful, no matter how abhorrent the denial may be.

References

Collins, F. S. (2024, September 22). Facts matter, and they don't care how you feel. *New York Times.* https://www.nytimes.com/2024/09/20/opinion/covid-vaccines-truth-life-death.html?smid=nytcore-ios-share&referringSource=articleShare&sgrp=c-cb&ngrp=mnp&pvid=A8EF4D4E-D518-474D-8ECD-26DD1955ECEC

Sullins, A. (2024, September 17). Most accurate forecast: Phoenix's record-shattering streak of triple-digit days is finally over! *ABC 15.* https://www.abc15.com/weather/most-accurate-forecast-record-shattering-streak-of-triple-digit-days-finally-ends-today-in-phoenix

Allergies

Learning Objectives

- Learn to consider non-obvious explanations for the data.
- Learn to use diverse data sources while "thinking out of the box".

Scenario

Ms. Kenya is a teacher at Cujo Elementary School. She has a close relationship with her first-grade students. They feel free to talk to her and tell her about almost anything. It is an open-door policy. They come to her when things are bothering them and when something really good has happened in school or at home. There is usually a group of kids hanging around Ms. Kenya's desk throughout the day.

One day in class, Ms. Kenya notices that Zoey is a little withdrawn. She keeps a close eye on her throughout the morning. At recess Zoey still does not seem to be her energetic self. The students head to the cafeteria for lunch. Zoey is at her usual table with a group of close friends, Sally, Goldie, and Ellie. After lunch, the students return to the classroom. Ellie approaches Ms. Kenya and innocently says that something is not right with Zoey. She is even more withdrawn and lethargic.

Ms. Kenya approaches Zoey and asks if she is alright. Zoey shrugs and shakes her head but she does not open up. Ms. Kenya is trying to figure out if the problem is emotional, cognitive, medical, something happening at home, or something else. Ms. Kenya asks Zoey if she would like to visit the school nurse, Ms. Maya. At least a visit might rule out some possible explanations like not feeling well or eating something that did not agree with her. Her next step might be to call Zoey's parents and see if anything happened at home since she has not been quite right all day.

Discussion Questions

- Do you think Ms. Kenya took the right steps?
- What might be possible explanations to cause Zoey's situation?
- Should Ms. Kenya immediately have contacted Zoey's parents?
- Does it make a difference that Ellie approached Mr. Kenya about Zoey, rather than it coming directly from Zoey?
- Could something have happened at Zoey's home?
- Might she have had a medical reaction to something she ate or encountered in the school environment?
- Might she be reacting to something someone said to her?

Probing Questions

- Discuss the possible explanations for Zoey not feeling right. Medical? Emotional? Home circumstances? Cognitive? Something else?
- Discuss who are the right people to consult.
- Discuss the steps Ms. Kenya could and should take to isolate or eliminate possible explanations.
- Consider what other data or information might be helpful here.

Discussion of the Ethical Considerations

It is often difficult to determine what is happening with a student. There may be a variety of explanations, some of which may not be obvious or within the control of the educators. That is why it is important to consider all sorts of possible hypotheses. The student might not feel well due to a medical situation like an allergy, something the student ate, or was exposed to something such as a bug. The student might have had an issue at home. Perhaps there was parental discord or a fight with a sibling. An explanation would be an altercation with a friend or losing a beloved pet. Perhaps she did not sleep well. Each of these are plausible.

This is why teachers need to think out of the box and almost become part-time social workers or nurses to help figure out what is happening. They can seek help and consultation from the school psychologist or nurse. They may have to ask school officials to seek assistance from social services. The teacher can simply ask the student or contact the parents or guardians. This comes down to triangulating data sources to try and help the student.

References

Nothing relevant

Belief in Students

Learning Objectives

- Recognize that beliefs matter. In particular, the belief that all students can learn is an important habit of mind.
- Appreciate that students across the ability continuum deserve learning opportunities.

Scenario

Samuel Elementary School has an active program of collaborations among educators that includes data teams. The data teams convene every week to discuss student progress. Sometimes the teams meet in grade-based cohorts and other times the teams meet with a vertical orientation of grade bands.

At a weekly meeting, the vertical teams are convening. Ms. Lula is leading the team of third and fourth-grade teachers. The teachers begin looking at recent benchmark results as well as using other indices. Ms. Lula highlights certain students to discuss. Mr. Jasper and Mr. Pointy add in some names. Many of these students are those falling behind. Ms. Gabriella asks if anyone had Hank, Gilligan, or Reese as a student last yar and what strategies they might have used that were effective with them to aid in their progress. Ms. Misty has had no interactions with the students. Mr. Jasper comments about Reese, that he tries really hard but sometimes simply struggles. Mr. Simon pipes up and asks about Hank. His words are direct. Everything he tried with Hank failed to move the needle with him. Resources were directed elsewhere to students where a difference could be made, especially those students who were approaching proficiency. The convened teachers were visibly uncomfortable hearing this as their interpretation was that Hank could not learn and the teachers had given up on him. Ms. Lula asks the team if anyone else has had any other experiences with Hank and had insights beyond his academic performance. She asks if anyone has knowledge of Hank's home circumstances and if there is support there. She urges an open discussion about how Ms. Gabriella might better serve Hank.

Discussion Questions

- What do you think about the discussion?
- What is your position on the question, can all students learn?

Probing Questions

- Discuss the disposition in data literacy—the belief that all students can learn.
- Consider how instructional resources should be allocated.
- Consider the notion of "bubble kids."
- Discuss what other data sources the team could use to provide insights into how to address Hank's needs.

Discussion of the Ethical Considerations

It is important for teachers to believe that all students can learn. If they believe that certain students are hopeless, they may unconsciously communicate that to the students, at the risk of doing substantial harm. Similarly, if teachers recognize that some students are so advanced that they do not need attention, then that strategy also can lead to harmful consequences. All students deserve attention and respect, regardless of their strengths and weaknesses. The belief that all students can learn is a foundational disposition of data literacy, a habit of mind. To ignore some students to advantage others is just wrong.

In Hank's case, it is possible that there are mitigating explanations and the attention to diverse data sources beyond student performance could provide valuable insights. Such data could uncover a learning disability, a visual or auditory impairment, or something else. Diverse data could yield insights into a home environment situation that could be addressed through social services.

Teachers must be careful not to write off students, make assumptions about them, or fail to consider explanations for why certain students may be struggling.

References

Booher-Jennings, J. (2005). "Educational triage" and the Texas accountability system. *American Educational Research Journal, 42*(2), 231–68.

Mandinach, E. B. & Gummer, E. S. (2016b). *Data literacy for educators: Making it count in teacher preparation and practice.* Teachers College Press.

Expectations

Learning Objectives

- Understand the potentially harmful consequences of some actions as a teacher.
- Consider the ramifications that teachers' words, actions, and instructional strategies might have on subsets of students.

Scenario

Ms. Dolly is a music teacher at the Pumpkin Middle School. She tries very hard to instill the love of music in all of her students. She uses all sorts of musical genres to pique the interest of her students. She holds high expectations for everyone, even those who may not be "naturals". Poofy is a gifted instrumentalist. Jasmine aspires to sing in a group. She also sings in her church choir and has been trying out for competitions at the insistence of her parents.

Ms. Dolly asks each student to select their favorite piece of music and prepare to perform it, whether vocally or instrumentally. The music could be in any genre. Students are to first explain why they selected the particular piece and its relevance to them. Some students are really excited, others are not so enthusiastic. Some students actually groan at the idea of performing in public. Some students fear they will be ridiculed.

Reese is first up and does an amazing job on the drums. He recounts that his dad plays this piece so it has special meaning for him. Patience sings a beautiful song that reminds her of her grandmother. Dixie plays a short piece on the piano. It is the first song she learned in taking lessons. Now it is Jasmine's turn. She gets up slowly and is obviously uncomfortable. This strikes Ms. Dolly as odd as she knows Jasmine sings in her church choir. The performance is not great. Jasmine is off-key and she forgets some of the lyrics. Some students like Poofy snicker quietly at how bad it was. Jasmine is visibly embarrassed.

Discussion Questions

- What do you think of Ms. Dolly's assignment?
- Even with high expectations for all students, what risks are inherent in the assignment?

Probing Questions

- Discuss the potential harms that could ensure from this exercise.
- Discuss the kinds of expectations and pressures placed on the students from this assignment.

- Consider how Ms. Dolly could have presented the assignment to mitigate some of the possible risks to students with differing levels of proficiency.
- Discuss what expectations Jasmine might have had for herself and how they played out.
- Discuss how expectations and the kinds of assignments translate to other courses and the ramifications they might have on students' performance and self-worth.
- Discuss whether performance classes such as art, music, or physical education should be handled differently from the academic content courses.

Discussion of the Ethical Considerations

A key to effective education is to try and not position students for failure or embarrassment. Ms. Dolly might have considered in advance the potential consequences of the assignment. Teachers and students both bring expectations for performance to any activity, whether it is explicit or implicit. Oh, X is really talented. S/he will ace this. And Y may or may not excel. Students pressure themselves and they likely feel the expectations placed on them also by their teachers and their parents. This situation can readily lead to harmful consequences. The reverse can also be true. If teachers set the bar too low, there is an implied message to the students, and not a good one. Parents are complicit here as well. Too often one hears about a "tiger mom" who pushes the student too hard academically, athletically, musically, or in whatever the endeavor is where there are aspirations (aspirations of the parent or the child). Or the parent makes an off-handed comment that implies that the child is not going to succeed no matter what. Expectations have consequences.

There are many things that Ms. Dolly could have done differently here, particularly in laying out the ground rules for the assignment and the metrics for evaluation. Performance in areas such as art, music, and physical education may differ from the academic content areas. Teachers may struggle to find ways to help students who are less proficient. What could an art teacher do for students who simply cannot draw or who lack creativity? What can a physical education teacher do to help students who lack hand-eye coordination, are afraid of the water, or are simply klutzy? What can a music teacher do if students are completely tone deaf or have no rhythm? There must be work-arounds. Maybe Jasmine had performance anxiety. Maybe she did not like being evaluated by her classmates. Maybe she could not remember the lyrics, feel the rhythm, or simply went off-key. Maybe her expectations were too high based on pressure from her parents.

It is also possible that Ms. Dolly should not have put the student in a solo position. It is not dissimilar to a student who falls off a gymnastic apparatus, one who consistently strikes out, or one who cannot render a simple drawing. Perhaps Ms. Dolly should reconsider not only the assignment but also the evaluative metrics. Give credit for the selection and the rationale, not so much the performance. Not everyone can win a talent content and school should not be one.

References

Lane, K. L., Carter, E. W., Common, E., & Jordan, A. (2012). Teacher expectations for student performance: Lessons learned and implications for research and practice. In B. G. Cook, M. Tankersley, & T. Landrum (Eds.), *Classroom behavior, contexts, and interventions* (pp. 95–129). Emerald Group Publishing Limited.

Yamamoto, Y., & Holloway, S. D. (2010). Parental expectations and children's academic performance in sociocultural context. *Educational Psychology Review, 22*, 189–214.

Masking

Note about this scenario. Although masks are hopefully a thing of the past, there are lessons to be learned about how schools and districts adopted policies during the pandemic and how they used data and evidence to inform those decisions.

Learning Objectives

- Understand the pressures that central administrators may be under when making difficult and contentious decisions when there may be political pressure.

- Gain an appreciation for the difference between using data and evidence when there are conflicting views, even though one side may not be informed by evidence.
- Understand the ramifications of making decisions when failing to consider hard evidence.
- Understand the interplay between the political factor and the decision-making process.

Scenario

Dr. Houdini is the superintendent of the Digit School District. Like many districts, Digit grappled with how to adapt to virtual learning during the pandemic and then return to face-to-face instruction. Dr. Houdini had a great advisory panel of experts to help navigate the transition from classroom instruction to an online platform. He brought in technology experts and well as sought advice from instructional trainers. He needed to convene another advisory panel to inform decision-making about the return to the classroom. Dr. Houdini this time enlisted the advice of medical professionals and infectious disease specialists. He regularly visited the CDC website, the state department of education site, and other relevant sources. He wanted to know what the latest research was recommending. Sometimes he received conflicting information, especially from the state in contrast to the medical sites where he inferred that there was some political positioning going on.

Dr. Houdini and the panel made some decisions about vaccination requirements, masking, classroom spacing, safe transportation options, and other policies drawn from the recommendations found in the scientific studies. He took the proposals to his school board. For the most part, the board was in agreement. The objective was to keep students and staff safe and healthy.

Dr. Houdini presented the decided upon actions to the public at an open board meeting. There were a lot of people in attendance. He began the meeting by saying, this is about the safety of your children, our staff, and the community. Our decisions were based solely on the available scientific evidence. Changes will be made based on evolving data and evidence. Dr. Houdini got no farther into his remarks before chaos broke out in the meeting room. Shouts of threats were heard. One parent, Ms. Dottie, tried to help by saying that the district is trying their best while other parents shout over her. Comments about firing Dr. Houdini and the board were heard, as were sneers about being in a totalitarian situation with illegal controls being put into place. The meeting so dissolved into potential violence that the police had to be called.

Discussion Questions

- What do you think of the situation?
- What do you think Dr. Houdini should have done?
- What do you think about how Dr. Houdini and the advisors used the evidence?

Probing Questions

- Discuss whether you think Dr. Houdini made the right use of the scientific evidence.
- Discuss your thoughts if Dr. Houdini ignored the evidence and yielded to parental and political pressures. What might the safety ramifications have been?
- Discuss how you think educational leaders should balance the use of evidence versus other factors.

Discussion of the Ethical Considerations

The pandemic was perhaps one of the most difficult times for schools and district for many reasons. Educators had to learn on the fly how to deliver instruction virtually and had to ensure that the technology supported district needs. Teachers needed computers and software, the bandwidth to deliver instruction, and classroom management assistance in how to handle a completely virtual environment. Districts needed to provide electronic devices to students and make sure there was sufficient bandwidth, especially for students who lacked the technological infrastructure. Data privacy issues abounded and complicated matters. It was a hot mess for many districts. And for students, there was significant learning loss.

There were significant data ethics and data privacy issues that emerged while instruction was virtual. Educators had to consider issues around the use of cameras and violations of privacy as the cameras provided views of students' home environments. Educators had to contend with questions like, what happens if a there are signs of neglect, drug use, abuse or more based on views from the cameras? There was a lot to deal with.

Districts had to determine policy around vaccination. As the pandemic began to ease, districts were faced with the decision of when to return to face-to-face instruction and how to insure that students and staff were as safe as possible. Decisions included the spacing of desks and providing barriers around desks and workstations. Perhaps the most problematic and contentious issue was the requirement of masks. Masks had implications for health and safety, first and foremost, but it also impacted individuals in other ways. For example, if a student or teacher had a hearing impairment, masks prevented lipreading and made it very difficult for these individuals to capture words and conversations. District administrators were caught in a war between applying scientific evidence and yielding to what often were hostile and extremely vocal parents who were anti-mask. The level of hostility in some districts was so extreme that superintendents faced death threats and being removed. Many superintendents tried to use scientific evidence but it was a constantly changing landscape and politically charged.

References

Healy, J. (2021, September 1). Arizona banned school mask mandates. Now some kids are sick and parents are angry. *New York Times*. https://www.nytimes.com/2021/09/01/us/arizona-masks-covidd-doug-ducey.html

Kunichoff, Y., & Steinbach, A. (2021, September 25). COVID-19 outbreaks 3.5 times more likely in schools without mask mandates, report says. *Arizona Republic*. https://www.azcentral.com/story/news/local/arizona-education/2021/09/25/schools-without-mask-mandates-more-covid-outbreaks/5850189001/

Spitzer, M. (2020). Masked education? The benefits and burdens of wearing face masks in schools during the current Corona pandemic. *Trends in Neuroscience and Education, 20*, 1–8.

Wein, H. (2022, March 22). Mandatory masking in schools reduced Covid-19 cases. *NIH Research*. https://www.nih.gov/news-events/nih-research-matters/mandatory-masking-schools-reduced-covid-19-cases

Inconsistently Late

Learning Objectives

- Understand the need to take a whole child approach.
- Recognize that one data point (such as tardiness or absences) may not provide a complete picture of a situation.

Scenario

Rosie is a tenth grade student at Bosley High School. She is a good student and a member of the cheerleading squad. She also participates in an external cheerleading group that competes nationally. She is good and she is well-liked. The students take the competition seriously. They must attend practices and they also must maintain high academic standing, a stipulation by the coach, Ms. Pippa.

Mr. Boss is Rosie's homeroom teacher and also has her in his first period class. He begins to notice that Rosie has been late on a frequent basis. Sometimes she makes it to class, and sometimes she does not make it to school at all. Yet, Mr. Boss knows Rosie is a conscientious student and is maintaining her grades. But missing so much school is not like her. He is concerned.

Mr. Boss decides to speak with Rosie. He also speaks with Ms. Pippa to see if she has any insights. Ms. Pippa shares some information she has heard informally from other students and parents during practices and at competitions. Rosie's mother is a single parent. She has a new boyfriend and sometimes does not come home, leaving Rosie to fend for herself. Rosie therefore has no transportation to school.

Discussion Questions

- Do you think Mr. Boss was right to speak to Rosie? To Ms. Pippa?
- Do you think the "informal" information is enough to take action?
- What do you think should be Mr. Boss's next steps?

Probing Questions

- Discuss whether social services should be contacted.
- Discuss some of the ethical issues that emerged in this scenario.
- Discuss how the educators can best help the student.
- Consider what options a school has to reach beyond the school boundaries to provide assistance to a student in need.
- Discuss how the triangulation of different data sources could lead to actionable strategies.

Discussion of the Ethical Considerations

The tardiness or absences are indicators that something may be amiss with Rosie. Mr. Boss is astute to pick up on this. Asking some initial questions is a first step. There may be reasons for a student being late: oversleeping, laziness, illness, resistance to coming to school, no access to public transportation, no parental transportation, or something else. Depending on the sources of the problem, Mr. Boss can then ask school officials to engage the appropriate agencies to assist the student and/or the family. Rosie certainly is experiencing a transportation issue. But there may also be a case of neglect that requires investigation. The triangulation of the data here can assist the educators to determine what is happening and then guide then in developing a course of action to help the student.

Reference

Data Quality Campaign. (September 24, 2024). *Connect school and district leaders to the information they need to ensure that their students thrive.* https://dataqualitycampaign.org/wp-content/uploads/2024/09/DQC-Use-Case-K-12.pdf

Pressure

Learning Objectives

- Consider the ramifications of leaders applying too much pressure to teachers around metrics where they have little control.
- Understand how various measures of "success" may be used appropriately or used irresponsibly.

Scenario

Dr. Halle is the superintendent of the Gucci School District. The district is located in a fairly affluent community. The district also has pockets of low-income students. Gucci tries to provide effective services to all students regardless of socio-economic status, ethnicity, or background. Dr. Halle holds high standards for performance for all students. This is clear to every principal and teacher. In fact, the high standards have been interpreted by some educators as undue pressure to perform, even performance at any cost. Some teachers have noted offhandedly that Dr. Halle is bucking for a big promotion to a larger or more prominent district, so the pressure for him to look good resonates throughout the district. Dr. Halle has promised the community that new policies and practices that have been implemented will raise test scores, improve attendance and graduate rate, and decrease behavioral incidents. Most importantly for many parents, the new practices are geared toward having more students apply to and get accepted by prestigious universities.

Building principals meet with their teachers to discuss what practices they can put into place to improve performance on the targeted metrics. Some teachers are already concerned because they feel pressured to show improvement on metrics that are beyond their direct control. A group of teachers discuss how they might change how attendance is logged to the metric shows improvement. Some of the college counselors discuss how they might steer students to certain colleges to improve acceptance rates. They fully understand that if students apply to "reach" schools or too competitive institutions for which they are not qualified, the acceptance rate will suffer. So if they steer students to less competitive schools, the rate will improve. Discussion like this continue with the underlying theme of how to show success even if they have to find ways to manipulate the metrics.

Discussion Questions

- What do you think about high standards?
- What do you think may be the ramifications of high pressure to perform on leaders and teachers?

Probing Questions

- Discuss the balance between high standards and undue pressure.
- Consider what might be foundational issues around gaming the system.
- Discuss how the metrics are being manipulated.

Discussion of the Ethical Considerations

Holding high standards for district performance is a good thing unless the expectations are unreasonable or seemingly unattainable. If you set the bar too high, people may feel like it is an impossible task. People may fall into a learned helpless paradigm. If you set the bar too low, then it may feel insulting and not worthy of effort. It is a delicate balance to define realistic expectations that are motivational and attainable. Anything else may lead to some questionable practices.

There have been many instances of educators feeling pressured to game the system, all for different reasons. Some of these instances have received a great deal of media attention. Some have even been made into movies. Consider the Atlanta Cheating Scandal where educators changed answers on tests forms to improve scores and performance. Some educators were arrested, indicted, and convicted. Consider the Varsity Blues event where parents paid off individuals to secure admission for their children in certain colleges. Educators were involved, parents with involved, and an individual who masterminded the process to game the system. In at least one case, parents paid a surrogate to take the SAT for their children, pretending to be the students. Interestingly, the surrogate was in his 30s and did not look like a high school student, but was allowed into the testing area. Consider the movie, *Bad Education*, a depiction of an actual ethical scandal that occurred at a district on Long Island where the superintendent sought to manipulate metrics in addition to there being financial indiscretions.

Gaming the system comes in many forms and at all levels of the education system. It may be small-scale, like helping a single student with an assignment, or it may be much more systemic and broad-based. There is the pressure to look good on accountability metrics. Data are at the heart of the matter. They make the case for looking good or not. So educators must understand the ethical boundaries beyond which they should not cross.

References

Blinder, A. (2015, April). Atlanta educators convicted in school cheating scandal. *New York Times*. https://www.nytimes.com/2015/04/02/us/verdict-reached-in-atlanta-school-testing-trial.html

Chen, G. (2023, January). When teachers cheat: The standardized test controversy. *Public School Review*. https://www.publicschoolreview.com/blog/when-teachers-cheat-the-standardized-test-controversies

Hartocollis, A. (2021, October 8). Two parents convicted in the Varsity Blues admissions trial. *New York Times*. https://www.nytimes.com/2021/10/08/us/varsity-blues-trial-wilson-abdelaziz.html

Considering Consequences

Learning Objectives

- Understand the importance of considering the potential consequences of a decision.
- Understand that consequences can be intended or unintended.

Scenario

The Bruno School District is facing some very difficult decisions in their financial planning. There is a budget short fall and some programs will likely have to be cut. It is not an ideal situation but it is a reality. Dr. Frances meets with his financial director, Ms. Josephine who makes some recommendations for cuts. They also confer with the school board on how to minimize the impact on their community, the students, and the staff. Clearly, they cannot cut the main academic courses. They could eliminate courses such as music, the arts, and drivers' education. They could eliminate some smaller sports teams. They talk to some of the potentially affected teachers like Ms. Whispers from music and Coach Sandy from physical education. None of the options seem great. They consider what negative impacts there might be to the academic programs. They work out various scenarios and decide what they think is the least harmful. This would involve gutting the arts, music, and some sports, at least for the next fiscal year.

Discussion Questions

- What do you think of the deliberation process?
- Do you think Dr. Frances and Ms. Josephine sufficiently considered the potential harms.
- What data do you think they used to make their decisions?

Probing Questions

- Discuss what might be some unintended consequences that could result from this decision-making process.
- Discuss how Dr. Frances might consider some of the unintended consequences.
- Consider how decision-making may or may not be able to predict the targeted and intended outcomes, but also might be able to foresee the unintended.

Discussion of the Ethical Considerations

A big part of decision-making is being transparent about what data are being used and what analytic methods are applied to any decision. Correspondingly, the consequences of the decision-making process must be considered. Every decision yields an outcome. Some outcomes are intended, whereas others may be a complete surprise. In this scenario, the desired outcome is a budget cut with minimal harm and disruption to the educational practice, even though none of the options were desirable. What may not be predictable in this situation is the collateral damage to some students whose programs were eliminated. Take, for example, students who excel at art or music, their classes, band, or orchestra are not cut and they were hoping for scholarships to college. Or take, for example, students who participated in non-mainstream athletic teams, and were also relying on scholarships and have not alternative for participation. Research has shown that eliminating sports disproportionately disadvantages low-income students because they cannot afford external club sports, whereas students who have the means can pay to play, the cost of the equipment and club fees (Aspen Institute, 2019). This is an unintended consequence.

References

Aspen Institute. (2019). *State of play: Trends and developments in youth play.* https://www.aspeninstitute.org/wp-content/uploads/2019/10/2019_SOP_National_Final.pdf

Pandya, N. K. (2021). Disparities in youth sports and barriers to participation. *Current Reviews in Musculoskeletal Medicine, 14*(6), 441–446.

Richtel, M. (2023, March). Income gap becomes a physical-activity divide. *New York Times.* https://www.nytimes.com/2023/03/24/health/sports-physical-education-children.html

Trudeau, F. & Shepard, R. J. (2008). Physical education, school physical activity, school sports, and academic performance. *International Journal of Behavioral Nutrition and Physical Activity, 5*(10), 1–12.

Metrics Matter

Learning Objectives

- Understand the importance of using the right data or metrics for the particular decision.
- Understand that the "right" data for one decision may not be the best data for a different decision.
- Understand the issue of transparency in data use.

Scenario

The King School District uses state standardized test scores for a number of decisions. Of course the scores are reported for the required accountability purposes but they are also used for other purposes like the adoption of curricula, teacher evaluation, student placement, and instructional improvement. Typical of most standardized tests, they are administered in the spring with the scores returned months later. Some educators refer to the data as dead on arrival. That is, educators feel that the scores have little meaning for instructional improvement because the results are so delayed that they are no longer informative. Yet district administrators maintain that the results do yield meaningful information that can be applied to other decisions. They just are not sufficiently granular or timely to inform classroom practice.

Discussion Questions

- What do you think about the utility of such data when they might be more meaningful for some but not other decisions?
- Do you think it is realistic and valid that the same data can be used differently for different decisions?

Probing Questions

- Discuss what might be considered role-based data and decision-making.

- Discuss whether you think state standardized tests have the granularity to inform classroom decisions for instructional improvement.
- Discuss the validity of data collected months in advance to inform about student learning and performance months later.
- Discuss the issue of timeliness as a component of data quality.

Discussion of the Ethical Considerations

The fundamental principle of validity is that the data should be used for the intended purposes. State standardized test scores are mostly used as a required accountability metric but they are also used for other purposes rightly or wrongly. One can question if data collected, for example, in March have instructional validity in the next school year. Students change over that time frame. Surely such data can inform some kinds of decisions but might not that the timeliness or granularity to inform instructional modification.

When policymakers introduced the notion of adding these test scores to teacher evaluations, there was a great deal of debate. Should the scores be the sole metric on which teachers are evaluated? Are they a valid index for that purpose? What other data should be included? Does such a metric take into consideration the variation across classes and validly reflect teachers' impact? What if a teacher has a high-performing class where there might be a ceiling effect? What if a teacher has a challenged class where there may be room for improvement but scores remain low?

There have been some egregious misuses of standardized test scores as well. For example, test scores often appear in real estate promotions, that a district is high performing and therefore a location is a good place to live because of its schools. The scores are not a proxy for real estate values but are being used that way.

The lesson to be learned here is that educators must be transparent about what data are being used for what purposes. Hopefully they are being used for the intended kinds of decisions. This is validity.

Reference

Cronbach, L. J. (1984). *The essentials of educational testing* (4th ed.). Harper & Row.

They Know It

Learning Objectives

- Understand how to triangulate data.
- Learn to appreciate that a single index may not be a sufficiently valid indicator to measure a concept.
- Understand the concept of attribution.

Scenario

Eighth grade teachers at the Cash Middle School are grading a common assessment given across the classrooms. Mr. Eddie, Ms. Allie, and Mr. Moses are looking over the test papers. Mr. Eddie seems really perplexed and questions some of his students' responses. He says, Rex and Dusty both answered two items wrong but I have observed them in class and they have demonstrated their understanding of the concept. Both Ms. Allie and Mr. Moses shake their heads in agreement. They, too, have the same things among their students' papers. Ms. Allie adds a reverse example. She says, I am looking at Misty's paper. She has never gotten that concept correct in class, yet here she did. The teachers begin to discuss the differences between what they have observed in class and on assignments, in contrast to the assessment.

Discussion Questions

- What do you think of these observations?
- Should classroom performance weigh more heavily than the assessment or visa versa?

Probing Questions

- Discuss what evidence the teachers should use.
- Discuss whether the teachers should just disregard the students' classroom performance, in favor of only the common assessment.
- Discuss what might have caused the discrepancies.
- Discuss how the teachers should proceed in terms of the discrepancies in both directions.

Discussion of the Ethical Considerations

The measurement concepts of validity and reliability come into play here as well as a few other factors. Here we have the issue that the test scores conflict with other data that the teachers have observed in their classrooms. What should they believe and what should they do? Validity comes into play here about what indices best measure the targeted concepts. Should you give more weight to the fact that students have already demonstrated their knowledge in class or disregard those data? What about the reverse? The concept of reliability comes into play here as well. Triangulating on multiple measures helps to increase the reliability of results.

There are also some other considerations. Perhaps Rex and Dusty have test anxiety or had a bad day for some reason. They know their stuff but could not demonstrate that knowledge on the particular test items. Should Mr. Eddie talk to Rex and Dusty or perhaps give them another chance? Is that fair to other students? What are the potential harms here? Now consider Misty's case. She has not yet demonstrated that knowledge in class as she did on the test. There are at least two possible explanations. First, some students take longer than others to acquire the skill or knowledge. So maybe Misty finally grasped the concepts. Or second, perhaps Misty just guessed correctly.

Consider Bertrand and Marsh's (2015) work on attribution and the ramifications of attributing performance to student characteristics as opposed to other factors. For example, in this case, an appropriate attribution might be that the measurement instrument is not sufficiently sensitive to what has been taught, causing a lack of alignment across instruction to assessment to student performance.

Every student demonstrates their knowledge in different ways and through different demand characteristics of the tasks. Each student achieves proficiency at different rates. Teachers need to account for these individual differences. Triangulating data is important.

One can also consider what differences there might be in the level of the assessment. What if this was a high-stakes proficiency test or an assessment that was developed solely to inform instructional decision-making, to identify students' strengths and weaknesses? How would that influence how the test or individual item results could be used and with other data sources?

References

Bertrand, M. & Marsh, J. A. (2015). Teachers' sensemaking of data and implications for equity. *American Educational Research Journal, 52*(5), 861–893.

Cronbach, L. J. (1984). *The essentials of educational testing* (4th ed.). Harper & Row.

Metrics Made Public

Learning Objectives

- Learn about issues of data privacy.
- Learn to balance privacy issues despite the possible motivational impact.
- Learn to consider unintended consequences.

Scenario

Mr. Bennett, the Ash Middle School principal has put into place a strategy that he thinks will motivate students to excel. He wants teachers to post student work to highlight how well they are doing. In particular, he wants student work hung up for parent-teacher nights so parents can also examine their children's work. This could be a natural for art teachers to hang paintings but could be difficult for teachers in other disciplines like music and physical education. The physical education teachers adopt a modified approach. They hang lists of accomplishments, such as the number of laps swum, the number of miles ran, the number of reps, free throws made, and other metrics for various sports.

The policy went into place a few months ago. Some students have had issues with it, however, and some have even balked. Some of the unhappy students have approached teachers with their concerns and complaints. These students range from the highest performers to the lowest. Some students have expressed embarrassment. The lower scoring students have been mocked as being dumb or uncoordinated. The higher scoring students have been called nerds or jocks.

Because many of the assignments, like pieces or art, have names on them, other students are aware of each other's performance, even if there are not grades on the documents. For the physical education lists, it is clear who is excelling and who is not.

Mr. Bennett convenes a faculty meeting to get feedback from the teachers. What he thought would be a motivational strategy obviously had unintended consequences.

Discussion Questions

- What do you think of the policy?
- What are some of the policy's limitations?

Probing Questions

- Discuss the data privacy issue in the scenario.
- Discuss the intended and unintended consequences.
- Discuss the potential harms created by the policy.

Discussion of the Ethical Considerations

There are a number of considerations in this scenario despite the best intentions of Mr. Bennett. Finding creative ways to motivate students is a good thing, but not at the potential expense of some students. There is a potential for mocking and even bullying in this case by having students know how other students have performed. This is particularly consequential for the least adept at a given activity. There can be name calling and shaming. Those are unintended consequences that can lead to substantial harm for targeted students. Even for the high achieving students, they too could be the recipients of mocking.

Perhaps the most important issue here the violation of student data privacy. Having student work with ways to identify the student is wrong, especially if there are grades attached to documents. Posting lists, such as in the physical education classes also is problematic. The teachers could use ID numbers to organize the lists, but students would likely figure out who is on top and on the bottom.

There have always been issues around the hanging up of student work. The issue of using data walls has been a source of debate. There is a privacy component but there also is the emotional aspect that can cause embarrassment or worse. Educators must consider the potentials for harm first and foremost.

Reference

Harris, L., Wyatt-Smith, C., & Adie, L. (2020). Using data walls to display assessment results: A review of their affective impacts on teachers and students. *Teachers and Teaching, 26*(1), 50–66.

Attributions and Confirmation Bias

Learning Objectives
- Learn about the importance of confirmation bias.
- Learn how certain attributions can cause harmful consequences.

Scenario

Mr. Roger is an elementary school teacher who is the lead data coach for his school. The data team members convene to examine some recent benchmark assessments that are intended to provide insights into how the students currently are performing. The teachers pour over the results. They look at grade-level, class-level, and individual-level results. Some teachers discuss how other performance metrics weigh in. They note certain students and groups of students that have done well, others who are improving, and also others who are seemingly struggling. Mr. Roger urges the team members to look at the full range of performance and discuss strategies and next steps. Ms. Gracie Ann comments about a group of students who have not done well and wonders whether it is because they may have language limitations or learning challenges. Perhaps there is a message here. Ms. Bonnie considers if the test is not sufficiently sensitive to student learning. Mr. Roger brings the discussion full circle and asks how might instruction be modified to address the learning needs of all students.

Discussion Questions

- What do you think about the discussion?
- What is the underlying message in Mr. Roger's comments?

Probing Questions

- Discuss some of the potential harms of attributing performance to student characteristics.
- Discuss what might be effective strategies to address student needs.
- Discuss the concept of confirmation bias and attribution theory.

Discussion of the Ethical Considerations

The concept of attributions underlies this scenario. In a transformative article, Bertrand and Marsh (2015) describe the four kinds of attributions that they found teachers use to explain results. First, there are attributions to instruction that are controllable, unstable, and internal. This means that teachers can and should modify instruction based on the results of various student performance indices, and not simply reteach. Second, there are attributions to student understanding that are controllable, unstable, and external. Third, there are attributions to the test or assignment. These can be controllable or not, stable or not, and external or internal. Finally, there are attributions to student characteristics. These are uncontrollable, stable, and external. The fourth form is perhaps the most problematic and can cause ethical issues. If teachers resort to explaining poor performance on student characteristics such as language learners, disability, ethnicity, poverty, or other factors, they are using a deficit perspective that promotes negativity. It can cause shaming and blaming. Teachers must be mindful about this as potential harms can ensue. Instead, the most positive approach is the use of data to inform their instructional practices. Teachers can try to determine how to modify their instruction to best address the needs of all students.

References

Bertrand, M. & Marsh, J. A. (2015). Teachers' sensemaking of data and implications for equity. *American Educational Research Journal, 52*(5), 861–93.

Bertrand, M. & Marsh, J. A. (2021). How data-driven reform can drive deficit thinking. *Kappan, 102*, 35–9.

Productive Time

Learning Objectives

- Understand the importance of using data to determine next instructional steps or actions.
- Understand the potential harms of not individualizing instructional activities as meaningful learning opportunities.

Scenario

Mr. Kona is a middle school teacher who loves to engage his students using a variety of technologies. Many of his instructional activities occur online, whereas others may not require technology. Mr. Kona's students span the range of ability and performance levels. He is diligent about finding the most appropriate activities for each student based on their trajectories of progress. Sometimes, the technologies present activities through personalized learning to individual to each student's needs. Other times, Mr. Kona needs to assign something he thinks is more targeted to the specific learning needs.

Mr. Kona's class is working on a topic and he canvasses the room for how the students are doing. It looks like some students are struggling and are in need of extra support. Other students, such as Klaus, have blown through the work and are becoming restless or even disruptive. The remainder of the class is fully engaged. Mr. Kona senses that he needs to provide the extra support to those students who are struggling. He tries to figure out what to do with the remaining class time for the students who have completed their work. He does not ignore them but sort of suggests that they just look at their devices for the last 10 to 15 minutes of the class while he concentrates on the other students.

Discussion Questions

- What do you think about Mr. Kona's strategy?
- Do you think Mr. Kona's ideas are effective?
- What would you do?

Probing Questions

- Discuss the idea of productive versus unproductive time.
- Discuss how educators should figure out through data how to reach all students.
- Discuss the ethics of focusing on one group of students at the exclusion of others.
- Discuss the potential harms.

Discussion of the Ethical Considerations

All students need attention, regardless of where they are in the trajectory of learning. This is one of the things that makes teaching and classroom management so challenging. You may have a class of twenty-five to thirty students who are all in different places, have different learning styles, and may react to instructional strategies differently. For some, they believe that high achieving students do not require the same amount of attention. Wrong. These students' talents need to be nurtured as well. They should not be ignored, parked in the corner, or relegated to unproductive time. Teachers need to attend to the data that tell where all students are and to help the teachers identify what kinds of activities can help them help their students progress along a trajectory of learning.

Reference

Cronbach, L. S., & Snow, R. E. (1977). *Aptitudes and instructional methods: A handbook for research on interactions.* Irvington Publishers.

Feedback

Learning Objectives

- Learn how to give feedback or present results that reflect the data and the analytics.
- Understand that giving less than positive feedback must be done in a sensitive and constructive manner.
- Learn about cognitive fallacies such as cherry picking.

Scenario

Dr. Izzy is the superintendent for the Camo School District. He is preparing to make a presentation to his school board about the district's progress on various accountability metrics. It is important to him that it looks like there is improvement. He is being evaluated on the progress and so are the principals. Dr. Izzy flips through the synthesized data reports provided by Camo's data czar, Mr. Teddy, who has pulled data from the data warehouse. The analytics do not look good. Dr. Izzy considers asking the Mr. Teddy to rerun the reports using different analytics and even different data sources. He again looks at the reports and considers which metrics look moderately okay, in contrast to those that are definitely problematic. He looks at the metrics such as absentee rates, attendance, dropouts, transfers to charter school, incoming students from charters, graduation rate, collage admittance, and performance on state mandated assessments. Dr. Izzy tries to figure out a strategy that will put the best light on the district's performance, potentially by highlighting the best performing metrics, while minimizing or ignoring the others.

Discussion Questions

- What do you think about Dr. Izzy's strategies?
- Do you think Dr. Izzy engaged in cherry picking?

Probing Questions

- Discuss the premise of cherry picking and cognitive fallacies, more generally.
- Discuss how Dr. Izzy might have delivered the less than positive results to the school board in a constructive manner.
- Consider how best to provide feedback in a manner that balances the results, both positive and negative, in a legitimate way.

Discussion of the Ethical Considerations

There are a number of data ethics issues embedded in this scenario. First, a key skill in data literacy is being able to communicate with and about data in a valid manner. This means knowing the data and the analytics and presenting them fairly, whether negative or positive. It is never easy to communicate poor results but it must be done in a constructive and informative manner with a strategy to move forward. As the *Forum Guide to Data Ethics* (NFES, 2010) notes, it is essential to be accurate and not use bias or manipulation in reporting when the news is not positive. Just because the news is bad or something is not working as well as expected, there is no excuse to misrepresent the data or information.

Second, the fact that Dr. Izzy considered if the district data person could "manipulate" the data or the analytics to look better violates all sorts of ethical tenets. There is never an excuse to cook the books, so to speak.

Third, Dr. Izzy is guilty of at least one fundamental cognitive fallacy; that is, cherry picking. Cherry picking is when one selects data or results that knowingly will support the message one seeks to convey, while ignoring those that would provide alternative perspectives. Cherry picking is not uncommon, as it occurs in advertisements, skewed news reports, and most definitely in political campaigning. It is not a good practice, along with the use of other cognitive fallacies, such as availability bias, confirmation bias, using incomplete information, and subrogation.

References

Kahneman, D. (2011). *Thinking fast and slow*. Farrar, Straus, and Giroux.
Kahneman, D. & Tversky, A. (1996). On the reality of cognitive illusions. *Psychological Review, 103*(3), 582–591.

Embedded Messages

Learning Objectives

- Learn to look between the lines to understand your students.
- Recognize that the obvious may not tell the whole story.

Scenario

Ms. Esther is an elementary school teacher who prides herself on knowing what is happening with her students. The students, in turn, recognize that Ms. Esther cares and will often confide in her. She has been noticing some potentially concerning behavior of one of her students. Penny has written an essay that has some dark thoughts. Sydney has done some artwork that also shows some concerning images. Ms. Esther wonders what she should do. She consults some other teachers about the students. She wonders if she should talk to Penny and Sydney. Or talk to their parents. Ms. Esther goes back into her files to see if there are any other indications of problems with the two students. She does not want to over-react but she also does not want to ignore possible warning signs if the students are trying to send a message.

Discussion Questions

- What do you think Ms. Esther should do?
- What data might she collect?

Probing Questions

- Discuss whether mandated reporting applies in these situations or should more data be collected for a better determination.
- Discuss what might be happening with the students.
- Discuss with whom Ms. Esther might consult.
- Discuss if approaching the parents might be wise if there is any suspicion of abuse.

Discussion of the Ethical Considerations

Teachers are mandated reporters. They must report abuse or other problems if they suspect them. Yet it is problematic to raise concerns unnecessarily, especially if an inquiry is wrong and might cause potential harm. This is a delicate balance. What if there is abuse and it goes unreported? In this situation, the most prudent means might be for Ms. Esther to collect more data discretely. She has good rapport with her students. She could cautiously ask some questions, using the rapport to talk to Sydney and Penny. If the students provide little information, she could observe further, speak with school leadership, the school counselor, the nurse, or other educators to obtain their perspectives and guidance. Protecting the students is essential, using the premise of do no harm but being aware of the potential for potential harms.

Reference

McTavish, J. R., Kimber, M., Devries, K., Colombini, M., MacGregor, J. C., Wathen, C. N., & MacMillan, H. L. (2017). Mandated reporters' experiences with reporting child maltreatment: A meta-synthesis of qualitative studies. *BMJ Open*, *7*(10), e013942.

Challenge Assumptions and Interpretations

Learning Objectives

- Understand the importance of challenging statements or assumptions to determine validity and feasibility.
- Understand the difference between assumptions and evidence.

Scenario

Mr. Bernie is a data coach at the Biscuit Middle School. He works with grade-level teams and vertical teams that cross grades. The teams are committed to helping find effective instructional strategies to meet the need of all students across the entire continuum of performance. Mr. Bernie makes clear the belief that all students can learn and that data can help to provide insights into where students need to go and how to get there. The teachers are not to ignore the brightest or the most challenged students. Every student deserves attention according to their individual needs.

The data teams are committed to collaborative dialog and constructive discussions. One of the working tenets of the team meetings is to bring the data. Discussions use terms like, "I see in the data" or "My interpretations or conclusions from the data are". The teams do not use, "I think," I believe," or "I assume."

Discussion Questions

- What do you think about the way the data teams function?
- What do you think about the way data dialogues are structured?

Probing Questions

- Discuss why it is important to challenge assumptions.
- Discuss the positivity of this data culture.

Discussion of the Ethical Considerations

As noted in the scenario about Sanewashing, recall Judge Judy's words of wisdom. Don't pee on my foot and tell me it is raining. What she is saying is, tell the truth. Don't assume. Don't think. Don't believe. Instead, use facts and evidence. This scenario illustrates what is possible. Mr. Bernie has created a positive data culture where there is open dialogue that takes an asset-based perspective. It is grounded in two of fundamental dispositions of data literacy; the belief that all students can learn and the belief in the use of data. This scenario represents the responsible use of data in every way.

Reference

Mandinach, E. B. & Gummer, E. S. (2016b). *Data literacy for educators: Making it count in teacher preparation and practice.* Teachers College Press.

More Is Less

Learning Objectives

- Consider that in some instances, having too much data is not ideal.
- Consider that there are times when additional and targeted data are need to inform a decision.

Scenario

Dr. Piper is the principal of Java High School. Dr. Piper is a data nerd. She loves examining data and has a clear vision for her faculty that decisions much be based on data and evidence. She has created data teams, appointed data coaches, and has provided the needed resources to support data use in a trusting, open, and blameless environment. Dr. Piper models data use in all of her communications. Teachers are appreciative of the support. Basically Java has created an effective data culture where data use is expected and deeply enculturated.

The school's data warehouse, data dashboards, and learning management system contain a wealth of data that can inform decisions on all levels. Yet there are instances where the educators feel overwhelmed by the plethora of data. Teachers often do not have sufficient time to wade through all the data they have and might need. There simply is too much, especially when classrooms are constantly evolving situations. They have to triangulate among snapshot, longitudinal, observational, moment-to-moment, and other data. They must also triangulate quantitative and qualitative data as well as complex background and contextual data.

Dr. Piper, as the principal, also must use data. She must use synthesized data that have been transformed into information and reports. One of the roles of building leaders is to communicate using data to faculty, parents, central leaders, and other stakeholders. Dr. Piper understands a fundamental communication strategy; individuals receiving information can only take in two to three key points. It is therefore essential for Dr. Piper to use the data to communicate effectively, not bombard people with too much, and the communication must be at an appropriate level of simplicity and granularity.

Discussion Questions

- Do you believe in the premises, more is less and less is more?
- How would you handle being swamped by too much data?

Probing Questions

- Discuss what you think is the right amount to data.
- Discuss how you drill down to the essential data.

Discussion of the Ethical Considerations

One often hears the complaint from teachers that they are drowning in data, that there simply is too much and not enough time to examine the data. Too much data can overwhelm. Too little data can mispresent the situation. Finding the right balance is important but can be tricky. One of the suggested approaches in the IES practice guide on data is that educators must be able to identify the key data to inform a particular decision (Hamilton et al., 2009). Perhaps the best example comes from aviation. On April 11, 2024, I had the honor of hearing Ambassador Sullenberger talk. He was the US Airways pilot who landed his crippled plane on the Hudson River. He shared the cockpit video and voice recordings of the nearly four minutes from when his plane was struck by birds and when he landed the aircraft on the river. It is safe to say that the recordings were chilling. But what is so relevant here is the processes he used to make a life-defining decision under the worst possible crisis circumstances. He first commented about the need for clear communication, collaboration, critical thinking, and distributed leadership. But most relevant to data use and education was the need to wade through a morass of rapidly evolving data with which he was being bombarded and attend to only the most critical and informative. This gets to the crux of the issue. As a pilot, Sully was being confronted with so much data in real-time. It was beyond human comprehension. Yet, he and his co-pilot managed to take in the most essential data and figure out how to land the plane without loss of life. Less is more and more is less.

In this case, the premise fortunately worked. Hopefully educators are never confronted with such a crisis, but the general principle of data use remains. Determine the essential data, but be informed by other sources to supplement and inform as needed. And issue is knowing when to supplement and when you have enough.

References

Hamilton, L., Halverson, R., Jackson, S., Mandinach, E., Supovitz, J., & Wayman, J. (2009). *Using student achievement data to support instructional decision making* (NCEE 2009-4067). National Center for

Education Evaluation and Regional Assistance, Institute of Education Sciences, U.S. Department of Education. https://ies.ed.gov/ncee/wwc/Docs/PracticeGuide/dddm_pg_092909.

Sullenberger, C. (2024, April 11). *Arizona Speakers Series* [speech transcript]. https://arizonaspeakersseries.com/

Fitbits and Apple Watches

Learning Objectives

- Understand the potential harms that can result from an over-reliance on social media and technological apps.
- Consider what might be the unintended consequences of seemingly innocent activities and decisions.

Scenario

Educators at the Emperor Middle School decided to put in place a motivational activity for both teachers and students after the winter holidays. Leadership and faculty all bought into the policy and announced it once school resumed. Each teacher and student would be equipped with and asked to wear a Fitbit or Apple Watch for the month of January to log their physical activity. Teachers and students were organized into teams. There would be an awards assembly early in February to announce the winners and provide rewards. The intent was to motivate people to be more active and increase their fitness levels, which would have all sorts of positive benefits. The physical education teachers would help monitor and collect the data and put the data into spreadsheets so participants could monitor the competition. Students and teachers were responsible for taking the data off their personal devices and record them into logs. Points were to be allocated for various activities such as running, walking, swimming, biking, playing sports, or other kinds of activities.

As January progressed, the teachers embraced the activity as it would enhance both physical and emotional well-being. A by-product was the lose of the holiday gains. Most students seemed enthusiastic as well as it gave them to chance to use the devices. However, some students seemed particularly stressed. They felt pressed to do activities that were not comfortable for them. Some students started to get heckled when asked about what activities they had done.

As students turned in their weekly logs, Ms. Jinx, one of physical education teachers who was monitoring progress noted some inconsistencies in the data and asked some students to provide their devices so the teachers could reconcile the device data to the logs.

Discussion Questions

- What do you think of using the technologies to monitor activity?
- Are there any potential harms to these activities?

Probing Questions

- Consider if there are any student data privacy issues in this scenario.
- Discuss potential intended and unintended consequences.
- Discuss the kinds of data that are being collected and their benefits and challenges.

Discussion of the Ethical Considerations

The idea of motivating teachers and students to engage in physical activities is a good thing. Everyone is bombarded right after the holidays to join gyms, lose weight, and diet. So the intention here is good. Having individuals monitor their activities also have become a big thing. With the advent of the Fitbit then the Apple Watch, and other apps, individuals can monitor and log their steps, laps, times, calories burned and more. For example, I play competitive tennis. Almost all my teammates monitor and collect data from each match: calories, steps, and activity levels. My former organization used to run a challenge event each January for the staff to get active. There were points allotted for each activity and duration. The winning team would get to chose a charity to which a donation would be made. It was a win-win situation. It got people moving who otherwise would be sedentary and the charity would receive a donation. It also created some funny competitive situations. I was accused of double-dipping by working from my exercise bike! It was fun and effective.

These are intended consequences. What is unintended is the pressure some students apparently might feel to exercise. Some may have felt the need to log data that did not exist to look better. Falsifying data is just wrong but one can easily imagine why they might need to do that. What also could be an unintended consequence is the potential for cyberbullying or in-person bullying. Research has shown the harmful impacts of over-reliance on social media, a Fitbit being one example (Khalaf et al., 2023). It can lead to mental health issues, bullying, problems with academic performance, and even suicidal thoughts. Certainly students could be enthusiastic over the use of the technologies, but boundaries must be established. Looking too often at devices, trying to change data, or relying too heavily on the technology can lead to unfortunate outcomes and potential harms.

Reference

Khalaf, A. M., Alubied, A. A., Khalaf, A. M., & Rifaey, A. A. (2023). The impact of social media on the mental health of adolescents and young adults: A systematic review. *Cureus*, *15*(8), 1–10.

Blind Spots

Learning Objectives

- Understand the assets and problems that surround the use of advanced technologies to collect and analyze data.
- Recognize the possibility that technologies do not present a complete picture of students.

Scenario

The Smushe School District has adopted the use of advanced technologies to assist faculty in their teaching, learning, and assessment activities. The technologies are not meant to supplant teachers' expertise, but to supplement. The technologies are grounded in AI and use complex algorithms to present instructional activities and assess learner progress.

Smushe serves a diverse population of students. Some teachers, like Ms. Fido and Ms. Gigi have embraced the technologies, believing that they will have more time to concentrate on individual student needs, beyond the interface with the technologies. Other teachers are skeptical. They have concerns that the technologies will replace them. They also have concerns that their expertise, experience, and foremost, their knowledge of their students, will be diminished. They are also concerned about what data are being used by the technologies, perhaps to the exclusion or omission of important indices that can inform their understanding of the students.

Discussion Questions

- What do you think about the use or over-reliance of such advanced technologies?
- Do you think the teachers have a real concern about the algorithms?

Probing Questions

- Discuss how the algorithms might bias the teaching, learning, and assessment process.
- Discuss what data the technologies might miss.
- Discuss the need to adopt a whole child perspective and how this may be ignored by the technologies.

Discussion of the Ethical Considerations

Advanced technologies are grounded in the algorithms that determine many decisions. They are populated by large databases that may not be representative or reflective of the targeted students. The underlaying processes can lead to bias and potential harms to underrepresented students. The decisions are only as good as the algorithms and databases so the data may not capture a full range of constructs that can inform about the students. The technologies may be unable to assume a whole child perspective. They are where teachers' knowledge, experience, and expertise become essential. Effective teachers know to look beyond certain data to help explain performance, behavior, or whatever by adding context to help inform the situation and the decision.

References

Dieterle, E., Holland, B., & Dede, C. (2021). The cyclical effects of ethical decisions involving big data and digital learning platforms. In E. B. Mandinach & E. S. Gummer (Eds.), *The ethical use of data in education: Promoting responsible policies and practices* (pp. 198–215). Teachers College Press.

Mandinach, E. B. (2025). *Culturally responsive data literacy: An important construct for all educators.* Rowman & Littlefield.

Walrond, N. (2021). *Serving the whole person: Alignment and coherence for local education agencies.* WestEd.

Walrond, N. & Romer, N. (2021). *Serving the whole person: Alignment and coherence for state education agencies.* WestEd.

Second Chance

Learning Objectives

- Determine whether it might be right to accommodate students when their performance does not meet expectations.
- Learn to consider how the ends may justify the means in terms of instructional strategies and the use of data.

Scenario

Mr. Cappy teaches social studies at Mocha High School. He has always given his students some leeway if they have struggled with assignments. He wants his students to succeed, but only if the students put forth a legitimate amount of effort. He does not appreciate laziness or apathy. Mr. Cappy also tries to find creative ways to motivate his students.

Mr. Cappy asks his students to write an essay about what the Constitution means to them. He provides lots of resources and has some deep and engaging classroom discussions about the history of the Constitution. He asks the students to think about the topic because it is both timely and an essential component in the founding and functioning the government. He really wants the students to take the assignment seriously so that they understand how important the Constitution is to our country.

The students return their essays and Mr. Cappy begins reading them. Oakley has written a convincing essay about the meaning of democracy. Bijou's essay focuses on that the Constitution is outdated and was written with the input of only "old white guys." Marley's essay completely misses the point and looks like he put in no effort. Mr. Cappy reads on. He gets through half of the stack and is really disappointed. The students either have not taken seriously the assignment or have not grasped the importance of the topic.

Mr. Cappy considers his options. Has he not provided sufficient grounding about the topic? Is there something he has done or not done? He questions his instructional strategy based on the data from the essays. He also considers if the students have just blown off the topic as irrelevant and uninteresting. He addresses the class and expresses his disappointment. He expected more from the students. He asks them for feedback and then says that he is willing to give any student the opportunity to rewrite the essay as a second chance so it will not negatively impact their grades, but more importantly, so that they will try again to grasp the essence of the topic.

Discussion Questions

- What do you think of Mr. Cappy's internal deliberations?
- What do you think about his strategy to give students a second change?

Probing Questions

- Discuss how Mr. Cappy considered the reasons for the student performance?

- Discuss whether giving a second chance is reasonable, given that the data show that the students underperformed either because they did not get it or blew off the assignment.
- Discuss Mr. Cappy's thoughts about the attributions to the underperformance.

Discussion of the Ethical Considerations

This scenario considers attributions, expectations, and using data to understand the students with the objective of improving student performance. Mr. Cappy perhaps had too high expectations. It is possible that the instruction was not sufficiently targeted. It is possible that the students did not gravitate to the assignment or simply blew it off. If the latter, there should be consequences. Yet, Mr. Cappy's goal was to find a way to help the students learn about an important topic in social studies. He could reteach, using the same or different instructional strategies, but the former obviously did not work well. Perhaps some different instructional strategies might work. He could design a different assessment activity that might not or might better engage the students. He could just move past the topic altogether. Instead, Mr. Cappy decides to give his students the option for a second chance which will allow them to decide about their own destiny. He has now shifted the decision burden to the students.

Reference

Bertrand, M. & Marsh, J. A. (2015). Teachers' sensemaking of data and implications for equity. *American Educational Research Journal, 52*(5), 861–93.

7
Change Is Systemic—The Roles of Organizations and Agencies

Chapter Outline

Professional Organizations	173
Schools of Education	175
State Education Agencies	175
Local Education Agencies	177
Other Capacity Builders	177
Conclusion	179

Just as I have argued that the case for data literacy in education is systemic, so too is the implementation of data ethics in practice and capacity building in pre-service preparation and in-service training (Mandinach & Gummer, 2013, 2016b). For data literacy, the recommendation was for data literacy skills to be integrated into existing courses rather than as stand-alone courses so that the concept will become embedded in all practice rather than viewed as something tangential (Mandinach & Gummer, 2016b; Mandinach & Nunnaley, 2017). In contrast, Warnick and Silverman (2011) recommended that ethics be a focus of stand-alone courses, using real world examples and case studies. In a now quite dated study, Glanzer and Ream (2007) noted the dearth of ethics courses in pre-service curricula, even focusing on religious institutions, rather than all universities and colleges. Only 9 percent of teacher preparation curricula surveyed contained a professional ethics course, in contract to significantly more for business, social work, and nursing programs. Clearly attention needs to be given to both data literacy and data ethics.

Let us consider first the model of introducing data literacy into educator preparation and then extend to data ethics. There can be stand-alone courses or an integrated approach where the topic is embedded in existing curricula and courses. Stand-alone courses require a professor or instructor who can teach data literacy. Colleges of education do not always have such an individual. I have been criticized for making that comment, but data literacy is a specialized topic and not everyone has a background in it. Stand-alone courses take up space in an already packed curricula. Administrators may not deem the topic sufficiently important. Priorities may lie elsewhere. These reasons may be why almost all the attendees at the 2016 annual CAEP conference reported that the integrated approach was preferred (Mandinach & Nunnaley, 2017). Only one of the nearly 2,000 respondents disagreed. The integration of data literacy can be applied in methods, content, and practica. Integration communicates a message that effective data literacy is an important and necessary part of educational practice. Yet integration is not without challenges. First, instructors must recognize the importance and be willing and able to apply data literacy concepts in their teaching. Second, instructors must find places in their courses where data literacy is a natural fit. Third, instructors need materials and guidance that allow for such integration. When we made this case over a decade ago, there were few materials and fewer instructors who could teach data literacy (Mandinach & Gummer, 2013). Data literacy, if taught at all, most often was found in courses for administrators, not teacher candidates (Mandinach et al., 2015). There were many hurdles. It is difficult to say how much progress has been made in schools of education to date.

There must be many cooperating partners to address the development of educator capacity for data ethics and data literacy, more generally. The data literacy book (Mandinach & Gummer, 2016b), outlined a systemic perspective of the agencies and institutions that play critical roles in the incorporation of data literacy into practice. This systemic approach was updated in terms of culturally responsive data literacy (Mandinach, 2025). Because data ethics are part of both data literacy and culturally responsive data literacy, the systems mapping is quite similar, but with some different

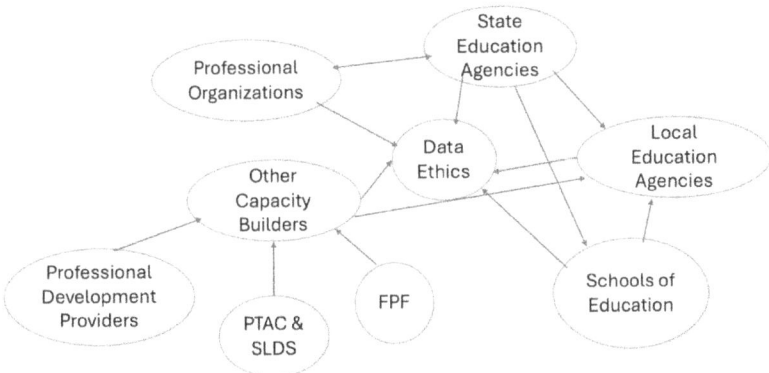

Figure 7.1 Systemic representation of the relevant organizations and institutions, created by the author.

agencies and emphases (see Figure 7.1). Thus, a discussion here is hopefully informative, especially for readers who have not seen the prior volumes.

There are some general categories of agencies where responsibilities may fall. First, professional organizations set standards for licensure and certification and inform state education agencies. Second, there are state education agencies that set policy for what knowledge and skills educators must acquire and demonstrate. Third, there are the institutions that are responsible for building and sustaining human capacity. These include colleges of education, professional development providers, local education agencies, and organizations that focus on topics such as data privacy. In the prior volumes, testing organizations were included because often what gets tested matters and therefore gets integrated into curricula and practice. However, the concept of data ethics is so specific that it is unlikely to be included in such tests, especially given how recently the topic has been added to standards such as the *MCEE*, as discussed in prior chapters.

Professional Organizations

As can be seen in the primer to the scenarios in Chapter 4, professional organizations can and must play a critical role in articulating the importance of the requisite skills and knowledge educators must have to be effective. NASDTEC, the Council of Chief State School Officers (CCSSO), and the Council for the Accreditation of Educator Preparation (CAEP) are essential participants, as well as the various professional organizations for educational leaders.

NASDTEC's (2023) *MCEE* specifically provides a code of ethics for educators so it would be a natural fit for data ethics to be included explicitly among the many principles. NASDTEC has made progress. As noted earlier, the 2015 edition of the *MCEE* did not include any mention of data, but the most recent version does. It includes references to data and data ethics, making a statement that there is a growing recognition about the importance of appropriate data use in practice. The specific inclusions are outlined in Chapter 4.

CCSSO (2013) published the InTASC Standards. Among the ten standards as noted in Chapter 4, there are a number of performances, knowledge, and dispositions that relate to data ethics. Standard 9 is entitled Professional Learning and Ethical Practice. It contains six performances, five essential knowledge items, and four essential dispositions. Only one knowledge item directly mentions data. The remaining items deal with professionalism and other aspects of practice. CCSSO is an important organization and their communications and resources matter. An explicit inclusion among the many standards and subparts would provide an important message to the field about the expectation for data ethics in professional performance.

CAEP focuses on educator preparation programs. Their standards (CAEP, 2022) help to provide guidance to educator preparation programs about the knowledge and skills candidates need to acquire through the curricula as well as topics such as recruitment, program impact, finance, and quality assurance. Under Standard 1: Content and Pedagogical Knowledge, there is a substandard that deals with professional responsibility. It says "act ethically" and refers back to Standard 9 of InTASC (CCSSO, 2013). Because CAEP reaches many institutions and has professional standing, it could communicate a strong message by being more explicit about the importance of ethics beyond professionalism and acting ethically. The annual CAEP conference typically draws thousands of attendees. Messaging there just as we did in 2016 in a keynote about data literacy (Mandinach & Gummer, 2016a) could be impactful to raise awareness about data ethics.

Professional organizations can influence state education agencies and inform them about the importance of a topic such as data ethics. Certainly, both NASDTEC and CCSSO have representation in and from the states. The professional organizations can influence what is taught in schools of education through their standards and messaging. For example, the National Education Association (n.d.) has a code of ethics but there is no mention of data across the two principles. This is a missed opportunity to expand beyond professionalism to other critical skill sets and knowledge.

Schools of Education

Schools of education can play a key role in developing an appreciation for and understanding of data ethics. Mandinach and Gummer (2013) called for schools of education to address data literacy in their curricula and then Gummer and colleagues (2021) explored how the institutions might address data ethics. Glanzer and Ream (2007) noted sparse coverage of ethics more generally even in religious institutions. There is a lot that the institutions can do by integrating the principles of data ethics in courses across the curricula and in practica where the concepts can be reinforced in practice. Just as we found about data literacy (Mandinach et al., 2015), there are conditions that need to be met to bring this effort to fruition. There must be professors and instructions who are knowledgeable about the topic. They must find room and places where the topic fits. And there must be materials that are easily adaptable and can be integrated into existing courses.

Because of the systemic nature of the integration process, schools of education must see the need to address the topic. This can be done through the inclusion of the topic in standards or through messaging from state education agencies and professional organizations. The need can also arise from the districts where their candidates and graduates practice.

State Education Agencies

State education agencies have a major role to play in determining what skills educators must demonstrate. The agencies develop standards for certification and licensure that specify requisite skills and knowledge. Surveys have been conducted about how, for example, culturally responsive practices (Muniz, 2019) and data literacy (Mandinach et al., 2017; Mandinach et al., 2015) are reflected in state standards. The inclusion or exclusion of a topic within the standards communicates to the education field whether skills or a knowledge set is deemed important. Such explicit messaging is essential as it tells schools of education and local education agencies what is important and necessary for effective practice.

As noted in Chapter 4, most states have codes of ethics for educators and several abdicate to the *MCEE*. Few codes mention data. When the codes do address data, it is most often about the disclosure of information or protecting confidentiality. Some states are more explicit. New Jersey mentions the ethical use of data, information, and research in ethical practice as well as the ethical use of technology. Michigan mentions the responsible use of data and evidence to inform practice. Arizona and Colorado include the use of diverse data in an ethics standard about how to use data. Ohio focuses on the appropriate use of technology with concerns about online bullying and social media. Yet, there are many missed opportunities. For example, Rhode Island and the District of Columbia both have data standards but say nothing about ethical use.

Staff from state agencies participate in NASDTEC. The superintendent or chief state school officer participates at CCSSO. So there are direct links to professional organizations. State agencies also are a conduit to the US Department of Education as well as to local education agencies. Their policies resonate not only to school districts but also to schools of education. For example, The Arizona Department of Education created a rubric around data literacy that all of the state's schools of education had to address through their curricula.

Thus, there are many things that state agencies can do to bring awareness to and recognize the importance of data ethics. First and foremost, data ethics can be explicitly included in the requirement for educators. They can work with schools of education by stipulating that the topic be included in preparation programs. They could require school districts to include data ethics, especially data privacy, in training or part of the onboarding process.

Local Education Agencies

School districts are at the heart of the effort to use data effectively and responsibly. They must create a data culture where effective and responsible data use is expected. Part of the enculturation is the provision to develop educator capacity through the growth of skills and knowledge. This can be done through targeted professional development and in-service training opportunities. Districts can require educators to demonstrate their understanding, at the very least, of data privacy through an onboarding process and subsequently sustained periodically thereafter. Leaders can model appropriate data use and communicate the importance through a vision statement and expectations.

Districts play a key role in the systemic nature of embedding data ethics. Districts must comply with state policies but they can also communicate to the state agencies and to schools of education skills and knowledge that bubble up as important to practice, such as data ethics. Districts hire professional development providers to enhance educators' knowledge. Therefore, the providers must be able to react to and address the needs of the districts.

Other Capacity Builders

Much human capacity can and should be developed in pre-service and graduate programs in schools of education. Professional development providers play a crucial role once educators are in practice. There are other resources that can assist in building capacity. Some reside with the federal government and others at non-profit organizations.

Professional Development Providers

When the data ethics book (Mandinach & Gummer, 2021b) was being developed, a chapter was included about the roles of professional development providers (Mandinach & Nunnaley, 2021). In preparation for writing that piece, I surveyed existing materials and guides on data-driven decision-making and reached out to the directors of two of the major professional development programs, Using Data (Love et al., 2008) and Data Wise (Boudett et al., 2006). The objective of this exercise was to determine if data ethics were included in any of the resources. None of the printed materials addressed data ethics explicitly or implicitly. Discussions with the two providers yielded a slightly better result. Neither program explicitly addresses data ethics, but they do implicitly espouse appropriate data use. Because of these findings, the Mandinach and Nunnaley (2021) chapter outlined actionable recommendations for how data ethics can be incorporated into professional development for data use. One of the recommendations extends past those providers to also include data ethics in generic professional development. Data use underlies most, if not all, professional development so it seems a natural fit to embed the topic within those trainings.

One of the challenges to this effort is how to help professional development providers find places within their programs for the integration of data ethics. Another challenge is helping the providers to effectively teach about the topic. Another challenge is the existence or lack thereof of materials that can be used. It is my hope that the scenarios in this volume can fill that void, as well as the data privacy scenarios produced for FPF. A final challenge is recognition by school districts of the need to enculturate data ethics in practice. If districts do not perceive a need, it is unlikely that professional development providers will respond and modify their materials.

Federal Governmental Agencies: SLDS and PTAC

The US Department of Education has two sites that specialize in issues around data and privacy. The broader site is the SLDS Grants Program (https://nces.ed.gov/Programs/SLDS/). Originally the SLDS work focused on building the technological infrastructure for state education agencies, but over the years, its scope has broadened. The website provides a wealth of resources about various aspects of data use. The site contains best practices guides. Interestingly though, none of the materials relate to data ethics. Associated with the Grants Program, there is a provision for technical assistance by the SLDS State Support Team.

The more focused site is for PTAC (https://studentprivacy.ed.gov/). PTAC provides training and technical assistance to education agencies around data privacy. It too, has many informative resources. Staff members can provide virtual and in-person assistance to school districts.

These two agencies could extend their resources to include not just data privacy, but some consideration around the ethical aspects of privacy and data use more generally. The inclusion of data ethics could help educators to use data more responsibly.

Independent Organizations Focusing on Data and Data Privacy—FPF

FPF (https://fpf.org/) focuses on data privacy in many venues and has produced a wealth of valuable resources. These resources focus primarily on data privacy, but some have also addressed data ethics. I worked with FPF on two sets of scenarios, the first for teachers (Mandinach & Cotto, 2021; Mandinach et al., 2021) and the second for leaders (Mandinach et al., 2023a, 2023b). The objectives for these materials was to provide resources for schools of education, professional development providers, and individuals around data privacy. Each scenario presented an authentic situation where data privacy and data ethics loomed large. They explored the actions and consequences, helping users to consider the implications for possible violations. They explained the complexities around FERPA and other regulations.

FPF's website in not a likely source of information for educators. The organization could do a better job of outreach to the educational community to build awareness and broaden dissemination.

Conclusion

It is safe to say that achieving broad awareness of and the capacity for data ethics is a complex and systemic issue. There are a lot of organizations involved here to make this happen. Awareness comes first. Cooperation among the organizations is essential. Unfortunately the need may come from very public violations around data ethics that not only may bring awareness to the topic but force the hands of the various educational organizations to address the problem. Ideally, pro-active action to build human capacity and knowledge would be a more beneficial strategy,

8

What Needs to Happen— Actionable Next Steps: A Recap

Chapter Outline

Recommendations	182
Awareness	183
Human Capacity	183
Educational Philosophy	185
Analytics	185
Theoretical Framework	185
Beyond the Framework	186
Other Considerations	187
Concluding Thoughts	187

This volume has covered a great deal of territory. It has introduced the constructs of data literacy for teachers and culturally responsive data literacy. It then transitioned into data ethics, what the concept is, how it is part of data literacy, and why it is important. A framework for data ethics was presented that emphasizes the key components of transparency and consequences. Understanding what goes into the decision-making process and the potential consequences is of the utmost importance. The two components are impacted by technical, social, philosophical, and political factors. Thus, data-driven decisions are not typically made in isolation.

AI was introduced as an emerging issue in data ethics. AI can provide a wealth of data and analytics not typically available. However, AI can be a threat to data use. With the advent of technologies that rely on potentially biased datasets and algorithms, the resulting decisions can be problematic and flawed.

The volume provided the landscape of how state and federal standards and codes of ethics address data ethics, or fail to do so. Such documentation is an indication that data ethics are prioritized as part of educators' repertoires. Then the volume presented a number of scenarios that can be used to help educators develop and understand data ethics, based on authentic situations that educators might encounter. Finally, the volume attempted to illustrate how complex and systemic the change process is, noting the roles of various organizations and agencies that can and must impact the enculturation of data ethics in educational practice. The integration of data ethics is a complex enterprise, as has been explored and explicated throughout this volume. There are many moving parts, and many things need to happen to make the integration possible.

There is no question that the enculturation of something like data ethics is and will be a complex enterprise. It will require buy-in, support, knowledge, and time. The following recommendations should be considered guideposts to effecting change. The recommendations and questions hopefully will stimulate thought and awareness of why data ethics are important and how to imbed the concept into practice.

Recommendations

There are many recommendations for action to make the integration of data ethics possible. These recommendations bubble up from the prior chapters. They reflect the realities and challenges of practice. They are also culled from the various chapters of the prior data ethics book (Mandinach & Gummer, 2021b, 2021c) as well as the data ethics framework article (Mandinach & Gummer, 2025). The recommendations are intended to promote enculturation of data ethics into educational practice. As noted in the prior chapters, many of these recommendations rely on various stakeholder groups and organizations stepping up to do their part. Change is systemic and complex. Foremost, change requires awareness, human capacity, prioritization, as well as other components of the infrastructure being in place.

Awareness

Perhaps the most important challenge is to build awareness of the importance of using data responsibly and the consequences of not doing so. There is an assumption that all educators act ethically, but some things are not clear-cut and must be made explicit in terms of how to use data appropriately. Awareness is the first step toward action. Awareness must occur across stakeholder groups, perhaps bubbling up from schools and districts. This seems like a deficit statement, but if there are enough ethical issues and violations, not just around FERPA and data privacy, but ethics more broadly construed, then educators will come to realize how essential data ethics are. Other stakeholder groups will follow, including professional development providers, schools of education, state education agencies, and other professional organizations.

Messaging is also important here. Having an explicit vision or rationale about data ethics is critical. Educators must know why data ethics are important, what are typical violations, and what are the potential impacts such violations might have on practice.

Human Capacity

As I have said repeatedly throughout this volume, it is imperative for educators to know how to use data effectively and responsibly. This requires finding ways to build human capacity and educator knowledge. Obviously, the key players here are schools of education, professional development providers, and in-service trainers. The impetus, or stimuli, are changes in standards and codes of ethics, as well as foundational needs from practice. Schools of education can and must begin to integrate data ethics into their curricula. Data-related professional development providers as well as generic professional development must include the concept into their work. Similarly, local in-service trainers should do the same. Much of what educators do relies on the accumulation of data almost every moment of the school day. It should not be hard to find examples for such integration. Local education agencies can implement guidelines and provide explicit visions for appropriate data use. They must set expectations and model good data use.

Materials must be developed that can be used by stakeholders. Materials should include good and bad examples. This volume and the data privacy scenarios (Mandinach & Cotto, 2021; Mandinach et al., 2023a) are a starting point. It is important for the materials to communicate several things. First, they must expand the notion of what data are. Second, they must communicate what good data practice looks like. Third, they must help educators build the needed infrastructure around good data use. This includes having an establishing data culture, sound leadership, the necessary resources, creating a data team and appointing data coaches, stressing the importance of collaborative inquiry, setting realistic expectations for data use, and creating a trusting environment without shaming and blaming. It also means ensuring that all educators have foundational data literacy. This may require assuming some risks with an eye toward long-term benefits.

For professional development providers, there are a few recommendations. First, it is necessary to find natural places in their materials where data ethics can be integrated. Second, there is a need to build awareness by discussing and differentiating appropriate and inappropriate actions. Third, it would be helpful to identify good and bad examples to illustrate responsible data use.

Gummer and colleagues (2021) outline specific recommendations for educator preparation programs. They identify several key actions programs can take:

- Teach beyond technical knowledge.
- Teach responsibility.
- Teach teamwork.
- Use case studies, tabletop exercises, and applied data projects.
- develop and use simulations and use cases that demonstrate data ethics; and
- integrate data ethics into both pre-service and post-graduate experiences.

Educational Philosophy

Mandinach and Jimerson (2021) considered the implications of data ethics across levels of school systems. Some of the recommendations focus on considerations and the philosophy of educational practice. First, data should be used to improve students rather than sort them. Second, data should be used as a roadmap to improvement. Data cannot tell educators everything they need to know, but they are guideposts. Third, data must be used for the intended purposes, not to inform unrelated decisions. This is a validity issue. Fourth, just as in the data literacy dispositions (Mandinach & Gummer, 2016b), data must support all students. Finally, data should not be used in terms of confirmation bias. Adding to these recommendations is an overarching strategy. Data should not be used in a punitive manner for shaming and blaming. Instead, data should be one of many strategies educators can and must use to improve and inform their practice.

Analytics

Dieterle and colleagues (2021) considered the role of technology in data ethics by developing a framework that focused on aspects of analytics that have created various kinds of divides (e.g., access, data, algorithmic, interpretation, and citizenship). Some of their recommendations are salient here. First, stakeholders should consider different forms of evidence. Second, decision-making must consider issues of equity and fairness. Third, new kinds of analytic methods should be considered. Fourth, consideration must be given to access, analyses, and interpretations for and by different stakeholder groups.

Theoretical Framework

The framework presented in Chapter 2 and in Mandinach and Gummer (2025) provides guidance on how to use data appropriately. Two primary recommendations result from the main components of the theoretical framework. First, it is essential for there to be complete transparency about the decision-making process. The transparency must focus on the rationale for data use, what data are to be used, what questions are being asked, what analytics are being applied, and the interpretations drawn from the process. The second recommendation follows directly. Educators must consider not only the intended consequences of the decision-making process, but even more importantly, recognize the potential harms and unintended and negative consequences.

Following from this is a need for educators to be aware of and consider how the four factors influence decision-making. Each of the four has the potential to create data ethics challenges. The technical factor can be seen in the use of the wrong data, flawed analytics, and inaccurate interpretations. The social factor can purposefully or inadvertently cause inequities. The philosophical factor can influence educators' foundational beliefs, not only around data use but education more generally. The political factor is perhaps the most challenging. There is no question that schools and districts function within a system of accountability. These pressures will not disappear and can cause good educators to do bad things. This is the foundation of ethics. These four factors create competing priorities and pressures that make education so complex.

It is my hope that the theoretical framework will encourage educators to think carefully about the components and factors that influence their practice. Paraphrasing from Mandinach and Gummer (2025), asking some questions could be informative. What is

- the purpose of the data use;
- the relevance of the data to the decision;
- the appropriateness of the analytics;
- the extent to which the interpretations are valid and make sense;
- the potential negative consequences and harms; and
- the impact of the four factors?

Beyond the Framework

The framework stresses the need to have a broad view of what responsible data use looks like. Just as Mandinach and Gummer (2021a) examined data ethics in terms of other disciplines, learning from good and bad examples of data use in those disciplines could be informative for educational practice. Medicine, journalism, business, law, advertising, sports, politics, and other areas can provide invaluable insights into how data can be used responsibly, as well as counterexamples of inappropriate use.

Other Considerations

Mandinach and Jimerson (2021) discuss the concept of positionality, "an intentional awareness of how one's own goals, aspirations, and expected benefits fit within the context of and subsequently affect any decisions made by the educator" (p. 103). The dispositions in the data literacy construct (Mandinach & Gummer, 2016b, 2016c) speak to this concept, especially the belief that all children can learn. Education is about helping all students maximize their potential to succeed. The belief that using data to inform this process works in parallel. Students are increasingly complex. They are more than a single data point to be sorted for accountability purposes. Context matters. Diverse data sources that provide a comprehensive picture of the students are important. Thus, educators should consider positionality in terms of their practice and the data that inform their decisions. Considerations such as these can provide a thorough and thoughtful foundation for sound decision-making.

Concluding Thoughts

As a researcher, I must be objective in the studies and work I do. That means using data, facts, information, and evidence to support the work. For over two decades, I have been studying various aspects of data-driven decision-making, starting with the technology that was being developed to support data use. Such development began with large data warehouses, learning management systems, and assessment systems. Since then, the field has blossomed into the development of dashboards and all sorts of applications that can be loaded on personal devices. As the technological infrastructure was evolving, the human capacity issue continued to be a secondary factor. Clearly, educators' capacity is fundamental. Educators are being bombarded every moment of every day with a plethora of diverse data sources. The key is to know what to do with the data. Thus, data literacy is essential. That means not only using data effectively but also responsibly. Educators will continue to be confronted with lots of data, some of which they may not even recognize as educational data and some that are not actionable, hence the need to consider the whole child. They will continue to be challenged by accountability pressures. These pressures will not go away. But every educator wants their students, classes, schools, and districts to succeed. The definition of success may differ across educational levels and, in fact, may present competing priorities. The metrics used to measure success may differ. Or the same metrics may be used and interpreted from differing perspectives, dependent on the role of the users. Students are the heart of education. It is about helping them to learn, function effectively, and succeed beyond their educational experiences. The trajectory of success will look different for every student. Diverse data will help educators along the path to achieving success.

It is my hope that this volume will help to move the needle, that educators will accept the challenge to recognize and incorporate data ethics into their practice. Data are worth using to inform educational practice. But there are limitations, and data are only as good as they are used appropriately and for the right purposes. Let all educators accept the premise and make data ethics foundational to what they do. It is a challenge worthy of a profession that is and can be so impactful for all students. Use data, but use data effectively and appropriately. Be a role model for data ethics!

References

Alwahaby, H. & Cukurova, M. (2024). Navigating the ethical landscape of multimodal learning analytics: A guiding framework. In S. Caballe, J. Casas-Roma, & J. Conesa (Eds.), *Ethics in online AI-based systems* (pp. 25–53). Academic Press.

AASA. (2007). *Code of ethics*. School Superintendents Association. https://www.aasa.org/about-aasa/Code-of-Ethics

American Statistical Association. (2022). *Ethical guidelines for statistical practice*. https://www.amstat.org/docs/default-source/amstat-documents/ethicalguidelines.pdf?Status=Master&sfvrsn=bdeeafdd_6/

Aspen Institute. (2019). *State of play: Trends and developments in youth play*. https://www.aspeninstitute.org/wp-content/uploads/2019/10/2019_SOP_National_Final.pdf

Bedi, N. & McGrory, K. (2020, November 19). Pasco's sheriff uses grades and abuse histories to label schoolchildren potential criminals: The kids and their parents don't know. *Tampa Bay Times*. https://projects.tampabay.com/projects/2020/investigations/police-pasco-sheriff-targeted/school-data/

Bergstrom, C. T. & West, J. D. (2020). *Calling bullshit: The art of skepticism in a data-driven world*. Random House.

Bertrand, M. & Marsh, J. A. (2015). Teachers' sensemaking of data and implications for equity. *American Educational Research Journal, 52*(5), 861–93.

Bertrand, M. & Marsh, J. A. (2021). How data-driven reform can drive deficit thinking. *Kappan, 102*, 35–9.

Boudett, K. P., City, E. A., & Murnane, R. J. (Eds.). (2006). *Data Wise: A step-by-step guide to using assessment results to improve teaching and learning*. Harvard Education Press.

Bridgeman, B., Trapani, C., & Attali, Y. (2012). Comparison of human and machine scoring of essays: Differences by gender, ethnicity, and country. *Applied Measurement in Education, 25*(1), 27–40. https://doi.org/10.1080/08957347.2012.635502

Buck, T. E. (n. d.). What are the privacy implications of biometrics in K-12 schools? *EdTech*. https://www.azcentral.com/story/news/local/arizona

-education/2024/08/09/artificial-intelligence-facial-recognition-adopted-for-school-safety-arizona/74637433007/parents.html?smid=nytcore-ios-share&referringSource=articleShare

Cain, J. & Darwish, M. (2024, April, 14). Fast rise in AI nudes of teens has unprepared schools, legal systems scrambling for solutions. *The Columbian*. https://www.thedailynewsonline.com/news/fast-rise-in-ai-nudes-of-teens-has-unprepared-schools-legal-system-scrambling-for-solutions/article_bc0ea8d8-f8f2-11ee-a594-6b9b82eac046.html

Caraballo, A. (2022, February). Remote learning accidentally introduced a new danger for LGBTQ students. *Slate*. https://slate.com/technology/2022/02/remote-learning-danger-lgbtq-students.html

Chaudhry, M. A., Cukurova, M., & Luckin, R. (2022, July). A transparency index framework for AI in education. In *International conference on artificial intelligence in education* (pp. 195–8). Springer International Publishing.

Cohen, J. (2022). Excerpt from privacy, visibility, transparency, and exposure. In K. Martin (Ed.), *Ethics of data and analytics: Concepts and cases* (pp. 188–193). CRC Press.

Collins, F. S. (September 22, 2024). Facts matter, and they don't care how you feel. *New York Times*. https://www.nytimes.com/2024/09/20/opinion/covid-vaccines-truth-life-death.html?smid=nytcore-ios-share&referringSource=articleShare&sgrp=c-cb&ngrp=mnp&pvid=A8EF4D4E-D518-474D-8ECD-26DD1955ECEC

Cooper, A. (February 25, 2021). *Arizona speakers series* [Speech transcript]. https://arizonaseries.com

Council for the Accreditation of Educator Preparation. (2022). *2022 Initial level standards*. https://caepnet.org/~/media/Files/caep/standards/2022-initial-standards-1-pager-final.pdf?la=en

Council of Chief State School Officers. (2013). *InTASC model core teaching standards and learning progressions for teachers 1.0*. Interstate Teacher Assessment and Support Consortium. https://ccsso.org/sites/default/files/2017-12/2013_INTASC_Learning_Progressions_for_Teachers.pdf

Cronbach, L. J. (1988). Five perspectives on validity argument. In H. Wainer & H. Braun (Eds.), *Test validity* (pp. 3–17). Lawrence Erlbaum.

Darling, K. (November 7, 2024). *Arizona speakers series* [Speech transcript]. https://arizonaseries.com

Data Quality Campaign. (2014). *Teacher data literacy: It's about time*. https://dataqualitycampaign.org/wp-content/uploads/2016/03/DQC-Data-Literacy-Brief.pdf

Datnow, A., (2017). *Opening or closing doors for students? Equity and data-driven decision-making*. https://research.acer.edu.au/cgi/viewcontent.cgi?article=1317&context=research_conference

Datnow, A. & Park, V. (2018). Opening or closing doors for students? Equity and data use in schools. *Journal of Educational Change, 19*(2), 131–52.

Dieterle, E., Holland, B., & Dede, C. (2021). The cyclical effects of ethical decisions involving big data and digital learning platforms. In E. B. Mandinach & E. S. Gummer (Eds.), *The ethical use of data in education: Promoting responsible policies and practices* (pp. 198–215). Teachers College Press.

D'Souza, K. (September 18, 2024). Even as Chat GPT becomes ubiquitous, A.I. pioneers warn of existential risks. *EdSource News Brief*. https://edsource.org/updates/even-as-chatgpt-becomes-ubiquitous-a-i-pioneers-warn-of-existential-risks

Dugue, R. D. C. S., Placido, R. L., Monterio, E. L., et al., (2024). Artificial intelligence and teaching practice: Concepts, applications, and education challenges. *IOSR Journal of Business and Management, 10*(9), 24-30.

Ellenbogen, R. (May 4, 2021). Pasco school resource officers will no longer access student data. *Tampa Bay Times*. https://www.tampabay.com/news/pasco/2021/05/04/pasco-school-resource-officers-will-no-longer-access-student-data/

Georgopoulos, M., Oldfield, J., Nicolaou, M. S., Panagakis, Y., & Pantic, M. (2021). Mitigating demographic bias in facial datasets with style-based multi-attribute transfer. *International Journal of Computer Vision, 129*(7), 2288–2307.

Glanzer, P. L., & Ream, T. C. (2007). Has teacher education missed out on the "ethics boom"? A comparative study of ethics requirements and courses in professional majors of Christian colleges and universities. *Christian Higher Education, 6*(4), 271–288.

Gonzalez, D. (April 1, 2024). Laguna Beach HS investigating incident involving AI-generated nude photos of students. *ABC 7 Eyewitness News*. https://abc7.com/laguna-beach-high-school-investigating-incident-involving-ai-generated-nude-photos-of-students/14603765/

Gorski, P. C. & Pothini, S. G. (2018). *Case studies on diversity and social justice education* (2nd ed.). Routledge.

Gummer, E. S., Gibbs, N. P., & Dorn, S. (2021). The role of educator preparation programs to teach about the ethical use of data. In E. B. Mandinach & E. S. Gummer (Eds.), *The ethical use of data in education: Promoting responsible policies and practices* (pp. 144–72). Teachers College Press.

Hamilton, L., Halverson, R., Jackson, S., Mandinach, E., Supovitz, J., & Wayman, J. (2009). *Using student achievement data to support instructional decision making* (NCEE 2009-4067). National Center for Education Evaluation and Regional Assistance, Institute of Education Sciences, US Department of Education. https://ies.ed.gov/ncee/wwc/Docs/PracticeGuide/dddm_pg_092909.

Heintzelman, S. C. & Bathon, J. M. (2017). Caught on camera: Special education classrooms and video surveillance. *International Journal of Education Policy & Leadership, 12*(6), 1–16.

Holmes, W. (October, 2023). *The unintended consequences of artificial intelligence and education.* Education International.

Holmes, W. & Tuomi, I. (2022). State of the art and practice in AI in education. *European Journal of Education, 57*(4), 542–570.

Kavanaugh, J. & Rich, M. D. (2018). *Truth decay: An initial exploration of the diminishing role of facts and analysis in American public life.* RAND Corporation.

Khalaf, A. M., Alubied, A.A., Khalaf, A M., & Rifaey, A.A. (2023). The impact of social media on the mental health of adolescents and young adults: A systematic review. *Cureus, 15*(8), 1–10.

Khodaei, S., Padev, M., Abdelrazeq, A., & Isenhardt, I. (2024). Beyond data literacy in engineering education. *Ing.grid.* https://www.inggrid.org/article/id/3967/

Kovanovic, V., Vberg, O., Khosrave, H., & Ferguson, R. (2024). Skills and competencies for thriving in the age of generative AI: The role of learning analytics. *Journal of Learning Analytics, 11*(3), 1–6.

Labadze, L., Grigolia, M., & Machaidze, L. (2023). Role of AI chatbots in education: Systematic literature review. *International Journal of Educational Technology in Higher Education, 20*(1), 56.

Ladson-Billings, G. (1995). Toward a theory of culturally relevant pedagogy. *American Educational Research Journal, 32*(3), 465–91.

Lipstadt, D. E. (2006). *History on trial: My day in court with a Holocaust denier.* Harper Perennial.

Literat, I., Chang, Y. K., Eisman, J., & Gardner, J. (2021). LAMBOOZLED!: The design and development of a game-based approach to news literacy education. *Journal of Media Literacy Education, 12*(1), 56–66.

Lohr, S. (2023). Facial recognition is accurate, if you're a white guy. In K. Martin (Ed.), *Ethics of data and analytics: Concepts and cases* (pp. 143–47). CRC Press.

Love, N., Stiles, K. E., Mundry, S., & DiRanna, K. (2008). *The data coach's guide to improving learning for all students.* Corwin Press.

Mandinach, E. B. (2025). *Culturally responsive data literacy: An important construct for all educators.* Rowman & Littlefield.

Mandinach, E. B., Bocala, C., & Perrson, H. (2017). *Findings from the new review of state licensure documents.* WestEd.

Mandinach, E. B., & Cotto, J. (2021). *Student privacy primer.* Future for Privacy Forum and WestEd. https://studentprivacycompass.org/resource/student-privacy-primer/

Mandinach, E. B., Cotto, J., Rastrick, E., Siegl, J., Vance, A., & Wayman, J. C. (2021, October). *Student data privacy and data ethics scenarios: The scenarios.* Future for Privacy Forum and WestEd. https://studentprivacycompass.org/wp-content/uploads/2021/10/Student-Data-Privacy-Scenarios_Combined.pdf

Mandinach, E. B., Friedman, J. M., & Gummer, E. S. (2015). How can schools of education help to build educators' capacity to use data: A systemic view of the issue. *Teachers College Record, 117*(4), 1–50. http://www.tcrecord.org/PrintContent.asp?ContentID=17850

Mandinach, E. B., & Gummer, E. S. (2011). *The complexities of integrating data-driven decision making into professional preparation in schools of education: It's harder than you think.* CNA Education, Education Northwest, and WestEd.

Mandinach, E. B. & Gummer, E. S. (2013). A systemic view of implementing data literacy into educator preparation. *Educational Researcher, 42*(1), 30–7.

Mandinach, E. B. & Gummer, E. S. (2016a, September). *Data and educator preparation programs: Data for programmatic continuous improvement and data literacy for teachers.* Keynote address at the annual CAEP conference, Washington, DC.

Mandinach, E. B. & Gummer, E. S. (2016b). *Data literacy for educators: Making it count in teacher preparation and practice.* Teachers College Press.

Mandinach, E. B. & Gummer, E. S. (2016c). What does it mean for teachers to be data literate: Laying out the skills, knowledge, and dispositions. *Teaching and Teacher Education, 60,* 366–76.

Mandinach, E. B. & Gummer, E. S. (2021a). Data ethics: An introduction. In E. B. Mandinach & E. S. Gummer (Eds.), *The ethical use of data in education: Promoting responsible policies and practices* (pp. 1–32). Teachers College Press.

Mandinach, E. B. & Gummer, E. S. (Eds.). (2021b). *The ethical use of data in education: Promoting responsible policies and practices.* Teachers College Press.

Mandinach, E. B. & Gummer, E. S. (2021c). What does the future of data ethics look like. In E. B. Mandinach & E. S. Gummer (Eds.), *The ethical use of data in education: Promoting responsible policies and practices* (pp. 233–45). Teachers College Press.

Mandinach, E. B., & Gummer, E. S. (2025). Shining light on ethical uses of data in education: Emerging importance. *Teachers College Record, 127*(2), 141-162.

Mandinach, E. B. & Jimerson, J. B. (2021). The role of the classroom, school, and district to ensure the ethical use of data: It's more than just FERPA. In E. B. Mandinach & E. S. Gummer (Eds.), *The ethical use of data in education: Promoting responsible policies and practices* (pp. 101–24). Teachers College Press.

Mandinach, E. B., Jimerson, J. B., Siegl, J., & Sallay, D. (2023). *Student privacy primer for school leaders.* Future for Privacy Forum and WestEd. https://studentprivacycompass.org/wp-content/uploads/2023/07/Student-Data-Privacy-Primer-for-School-Leaders.pdf

Mandinach, E. B., Jimerson, J. B., Siegl, J., & Tebbenkamp, M. (2023b). *Student data privacy and data ethics scenarios for school leaders.* Future for Privacy Forum and WestEd. https://studentprivacycompass.org/wp-content/uploads/2023/07/Student-Data-Privacy-Scenarios.pdf

Mandinach, E. B. & Nunnaley, D. (2017). *Practitioner data literacy: Modules for teacher education.* WestEd.

Mandinach, E. B. & Nunnaley, D. (2021). The role of professional development providers in training data ethics. In E. B. Mandinach & E. S. Gummer (Eds.), *The ethical use of data in education: Promoting responsible policies and practices* (pp. 125–43). Teachers College Press.

Mandinach, E. B., Warner, S., & Mundry, S. E. (2019, November). *Using data to promote culturally responsive teaching* (webinar). US Department of Education, Institute of Education Sciences, National Center for Education Evaluation and Regional Assistance, Regional Educational Laboratory Northeast & Islands.

Martin, K. (Ed.). (2022a). *Ethics of data and analytics: Concepts and cases.* CRC Press.

Martin, K. (2022b). Transparency and accountability in data analytics. In K. Martin (Ed.), *Ethics of data and analytics: Concepts and cases* (pp. 403–407). CRC Press.

McGrory, K., & Weber, N. (2021, April 19). Feds investigating Pasco schools giving student data to sheriff. *Tampa Bay Times.* https://www.tampabay.com/investigations/2021/04/19/feds-investigating-pasco-schools-giving-student-data-to-sheriff/

McIntrye, L. (2018). *Post-truth*. MIT Press.
McIntyre, L. (2021). *How to talk to a science denier: Conversations with flat earthers, climate deniers, and other who defy reason*. MIT Press.
Messick, S. J. (1989). Validity. In. R. L. Linn (Ed.), *Educational measurement* (3rd ed., pp. 13–103). Macmillan Publishing Company.
Muniz, J. (2019). *Culturally responsive teaching: A 50-state survey of teaching standards*. https://www.newamerica.org/education-policy/reports/culturally-responsive-teaching/
National Association of Secondary School Principals. (n.d.). *Position statement: Ethics for school leaders*. Author. https://www.nassp.org/wp-content/uploads/2020/05/NASSP_position-statement_Ethics.pdf
National Association of State Directors of Teacher Education and Certification. (2015). *Model code of ethics for educators*. https://cdn.ymaws.com/www.nasdtec.net/resource/resmgr/mcee/changes_from_1st_to_2nd_ed.pdf
National Association of State Directors of Teacher Education and Certification. (2023). *Model code of ethics for educators*. https://www.nasdtec.net/page/MCEE_Doc
National Council of Teachers of English. (2013, April 20). *NCTE position statement on machine scoring*. https://ncte.org/statement/machine_scoring/
National Education Association. (n.d.). *Code of ethics for educators*. https://www.nea.org/resource-library/code-ethics-educators
National Forum on Educational Statistics. (2010). *Forum guide to data ethics* (NFES 2010–801). US Department of Education, National Center for Education Statistics. https://nces.ed.gov/pubs2010/2010801.pdf
National Forum on Educational Statistics. (2016). *Forum guide to data privacy* (NFES 2016–096). US Department of Education, National Center for Education Statistics. https://nces.ed.gov/pubs2016/NFES2016096
National Forum on Educational Statistics. (2021). *Forum guide to strategies for education data collection and reporting (SEDCAR)* (NFES 2021–013). US Department of Education, National Center for Education Statistics. https://nces.ed.gov/pubs2021/NFES2021013.pdf
National Forum on Educational Statistics. (2024). *Forum guide to data literacy* (NFES 2024–079). US Department of Education, National Center for Education Statistics. https://nces.ed.gov/Pubs2024/NFES2024079.pdf
National Forum on Educational Statistics. (2025). *Introduction to artificial intelligence: A Forum Guide for state and local education agencies* (NFES 2025). US Department of Education, National Center for Education Statistics.

National Policy Board for Educational Administration. (2015). *Professional standards for educational leaders*. Author. https://www.npbea.org/wp-content/uploads/2017/06/Professional-Standards-for-Educational-Leaders_2015.pdf

New York Office of Information Technology Services. (September 27, 2023). *State education department issues determination on biometric identifying technology in schools*. https://www.nysed.gov/news/2023/state-education-department-issues-determination-biometric-identifying-technology-schools

Nguyen, C. T. (2024, Winter). The limits of data. *Issues in Science and Technology, XL*(2), 94–101.

Nichols, S. L. (2021). Educational policy contexts and the (un)ethical use of data. In E. B. Mandinach & E. S. Gummer (Eds.), *The ethical use of data in education: Promoting responsible policies and practices* (pp. 81–97). Teachers College Press.

Pane, J., Steiner, E. D., Baird, M. D., & Hamilton, L. S. (2015, November). *Continued progress: Promising evidence on personalized learning*. Bill & Melinda Gates Foundation. file:///Users/emandin/Desktop/RAND_RR1365.pdf

Parrish, M. & Sullivan, N. (August 9, 2024a). AI, facial recognition security camera systems coming to Arizona schools. *Arizona Republic*. https://www.azcentral.com/story/news/local/arizona-education/2024/08/09/artificial-intelligence-facial-recognition-adopted-for-school-safety-arizona/74637433007/

Parrish, M. & Sullivan, N. (August 14, 2024b). Arizona schools embrace AI, facial recognition cameras. *Arizona Republic*. https://arizonarepublic-az.newsmemory.com/?token=581ae1b5e637d4982b78341caec9fb66&cnum=7646d942-26d2-e711-b65f-90b11c343abd&fod=1111111-0&selDate=20240906&licenseType=paid_subscriber&

Pinski, M. & Benlian, A. (2024). AI literacy for users – A comprehensive review and future research directions of learning methods, components, and effect. *Computer in Human Behavior: Artificial Humans*, 100062.

Ramineni, C., Trapani, C. S., Williamson, D. M., Davey, T. & Bridgeman, B. (2012), *Evaluation of the E-RATER® scoring engine for the TOEFL® independent and integrated prompts* (ETS Research Report Series, 2012: i-5)1. https://doi.org/10.1002/j.2333-8504.2012.tb02288.x

Reddy, A. (December 18, 2020). The trouble with Pasco County's predictive policing polies. *Student Privacy Compass*. https://studentprivacycompass.org/pasco/

Ritchie, E. I. (April 2, 2024). Laguna beach high investigating AI-generated inappropriate photos of students. *The Orange County Register*. https://

www.ocregister.com/2024/04/02/laguna-beach-high-investigating-ai-generated-inappropriate-photos-of-students/

Roberts, L. (November 29, 2021). Kari Lake's classroom camera idea isn't about accountability. It's about electability. *Arizona Republic.* https://www.azcentral.com/story/opinion/op-ed/laurieroberts/2021/11/29/kari-lake-classroom-camera-idea-votes-not-accountability/8798357002/

Rosenberg, J. M., Borchers, C., Burchfield, M. A., Anderson, D., Stegenga, S. M., & Fischer, C. (2022). Post about student on Facebook: A data ethics perspective. *Educational Researcher, 51*(8), 547–550.

Schermele, Z. (March 28, 2024). Students used AI to create nude photos of their classmates. For some, arrests came next. *USA Today.* https://www.usatoday.com/story/news/education/2024/03/28/ai-nudes-generate-chaos-at-schools/72976869007/

Schuessler, J., Hartocollis, A., Levenson, M., & Blinder, A. (January 2, 2024.). Harvard president resigns after mounting plagiarism accusations. *New York Times.* https://www.nytimes.com/2024/01/02/us/harvard-claudine-gay-resigns.html

Selingo, J. (2020). *Who gets in and why: A year inside college admissions.* Scribner.

Serna, I., Morales, A., Fierrez, J., Cebrian, M., Obradovich, N., & Rahwan, I. (2019). Algorithmic discrimination: Formulation and exploration in deep learning-based face biometrics. *arXiv preprint.* arXiv:1912.01842.

Sinatra, G. M., & Hofer, B. A. (2021). *Science denial: Why it happens and what to do about it.* Oxford.

Singer, N. (July 6, 2024). Students target teachers in group TikTok attack, shaking their school. *New York Times.* https://www.nytimes.com/2024/07/06/technology/tiktok-fake-teachers-pennsylvania.html

Singer, N. & Krolik, A. (May 9, 2021). Online cheating charges upend Dartmouth Medical School. *New York Times.* https://www.nytimes.com/2021/05/09/technology/dartmouth-geisel-medical-cheating.html

Smith, M. & Miller, S. (2022). The ethical application of biometric facial recognition technology. *AI & Society, 37*(1), 167–75.

Snipes, J. & Tran, L. (2015). *Early indicators and academic mindsets in the Clark County School District.* REL West@WestEd.

Statewide Longitudinal Data Systems Grants Program. (n.d.). *About the SLDS grants program.* https://nces.ed.gov/programs/slds/about_SLDS.asp

Sullenberger, C. (April 11, 2024). *Arizona speakers series* [speech transcript]. https://arizonaspeakersseries.com/

Toor, R. (2014). *Admissions confidential: An insider's account of the elite college selection process.* St. Martin's Press.

Vermont Agency of Education. (2021). *Vermont's education recovery: Framework and overview.* https://education.vermont.gov/sites/aoe/files/documents/edu-framework-vermonts-education-recovery.pdf

Wang, Y. (2919). Is data-driven decision making at odds with moral decision making? A critical review of school leaders' decision making in the era of school accountability. *Values and Ethics in Educational Administration, 14*(2), 1–8.

Warnick, B. R. & Silverman, S. K. (2011). A framework for professional ethics courses in teacher education. *Journal of Teacher Education, 62*(3), 273–285.

Williamson, B., Molnar, A., & Boninger, F. (March, 2024). *Time for a pause: Without effective public oversight, AI in schools will do more harm than good.* National Education Policy Center. /nepc.colorado.edu/publication/ai

Woodruff, J. (February 29, 2024). *Arizona speakers series* [Speech transcript]. https://arizonaseries.com

Index

accountability viii, ix, xi, 2, 3, 7, 8, 16, 18, 19, 24, 38, 52–4, 96, 104–6, 120, 131, 141, 142, 145, 146, 155, 186–8
analytics xi, 9, 12, 14–16, 18, 35–7, 52, 76, 88, 112, 144, 156, 157, 181, 182, 185, 186
artificial intelligence ix, xi, 14, 24–38, 90, 92, 93, 165–6, 182
asset/deficit modeling 18, 20, 21, 37, 153, 160, 183
assumptions 15, 16, 18, 22, 27, 37, 38, 50, 65–6, 88, 96, 123, 126, 131, 159–62, 183
attributions 20, 48, 117, 141, 148, 151–3, 159, 169
automated scoring 27–28, 92–4
awareness xii, 7, 13, 38, 174, 176, 179, 182–5

bias viii, 12, 18, 20, 22–6, 28–32, 37, 38, 45, 47, 48, 50, 69, 70, 76, 77, 86–8, 90, 92, 93, 117, 118, 122, 151, 152, 156, 157, 166, 182, 185
bullying/cyberbullying 46, 49, 72, 78–80, 97, 101, 119, 151, 165, 176

chatbots 30
classroom monitoring 33, 64, 67–8, 89–91
conceptual framework for data literacy 20–23
confirmation bias 38, 76, 86, 88, 151–3, 157, 185

consequences xii, 7, 9, 11, 14–18, 21–4, 26, 28, 31, 33, 34, 36, 37, 41, 43, 50–2, 66, 68, 90, 131, 133, 142–4, 150, 151, 165, 169, 179, 181, 183, 186
culturally responsive data literacy 20–23, 39, 50, 172, 181

data culture xii, 4, 12, 16, 120, 161, 177, 184
data-driven decision making viii, xi, xii, 1–4, 7–9, 12, 14–16, 18–20, 23, 24, 26, 30, 36, 37, 43, 48, 50, 52, 54, 66, 74, 88, 93, 95, 96, 111, 113, 135, 144, 147, 149, 160, 161, 177, 181, 182, 185–7
data ethics viii, ix, xi, xii, 1, 5–9, 11, 12, 14–24, 27, 34–6, 38, 40–2, 47–9, 86, 136, 156, 171–9, 182–8
data literacy viii, ix, xii, 3–5, 11–14, 16–24, 39, 40, 49, 50, 77, 131, 156, 158, 160, 171, 172, 174–6, 181, 184, 185, 187, 188
data privacy 5–7, 11–15, 21, 24, 27–9, 33–6, 39, 46, 47, 49, 64, 73, 90, 91, 97–101, 109, 111, 120, 136, 137, 151, 173, 176–9, 183
deepfakes 33–34, 50, 54, 71–3
denial viii, xii, 6, 53, 54, 74–8, 89, 125–7
dispositions/habits of mind 5, 11, 12, 14, 16, 17, 21, 23, 46, 47, 50, 131, 160, 174, 185, 187

early warning systems   30–31, 94–6
EdFacts   2
educator preparation programs   4, 5, 24, 171, 172, 174–6, 183, 184
evidence   viii, 1, 6, 7, 33, 43, 49, 50, 52, 64, 66, 68, 74–7, 87–9, 93, 107, 109, 122, 125, 126, 134–7, 148, 159–61, 176, 185, 187

facial and voice recognition   28–30, 69–70
FERPA   13–14, 38, 46, 49, 98, 103, 120, 179, 183
framework factors   16–18, 21–3, 52, 181–2, 186
framework for data ethics   xi-xii, 11, 12, 14–18, 23, 34, 36, 37, 51, 181, 182, 185–8

health apps   32–33, 102–3, 163–5
human capacity   12, 24, 28–30, 36–8, 94, 162–73, 177, 179, 183–4, 187–8

inquiry process   viii, 4, 16, 21, 23, 184
Institute of Education Sciences   1–3, 48

local education agencies   2, 14, 19, 44, 48, 173, 176, 177, 184

misinformation/disinformation   viii, 6, 24, 64, 76, 84–6, 109
Model Code of Ethics   xi, 6, 39, 41, 43–6, 48–50, 173, 174, 176

personalized learning   27
philosophy   185
plagiarism detection   31–32, 65, 122, 123

professional development
  providers   105, 173, 177–9, 183, 184
professional organizations   xi, 40, 173–5
professional standards   xi, 6, 12, 19, 40–9, 67, 173–6, 182, 183

recommendations   171–179, 181–8
reliability   15, 16, 28, 30, 36, 45, 52, 65, 76, 77, 113, 148

scenarios   39–41, 50, 53–169
social media   27, 45, 49, 72, 73, 76, 79, 80, 114–15, 165, 176
state education agencies   2, 14, 19, 44, 45, 48–50, 56, 135, 171, 173, 175–8, 183
Statewide Longitudinal Data Systems   2, 173, 178
systemic change   xii, 63, 106, 142, 171–9, 182, 183

technologies   viii, ix, xi, xii, 2–8, 22, 25–38, 43, 45–7, 49, 50, 70, 73, 84, 89–93, 102–3, 135, 136, 153, 154, 160, 163–7, 176, 178, 182, 185, 187
transparency   xii, 11, 12, 14–18, 21–4, 35, 36, 38, 43–5, 50–2, 106, 120, 144, 146, 181, 186

validity   ix, 15, 16, 30, 35, 36, 65, 91, 113, 146, 148, 185

whole child   9, 19, 20, 36, 48, 98, 138, 166–7, 188